DATE DUE

DEMCO 128-5046

COUNTRIES OF THE WORLD

Democratic Republic of the Congo

Gareth Stevens Publishing
A WORLD ALMANAC EDUCATION GROUP COMPANY

About the Author: Nina Kushner obtained her master's degree and master in philosophy in History from Columbia University in New York and is currently working on her doctorate. She has worked as a freelance journalist in Boston and New York.

PICTURE CREDITS
Léonie Abo / University of Western
   Australia: 29
A.N.A. Press Agency: 7
ANACCO: 82, 90
Archive Photos: 11, 37, 69, 77, 78,
   83 (both), 84
Camera Press: cover, 15 (both), 38, 68, 75
The Canadian Press Picture Archive: 14
   (David Guttenfelder), 16 (Blaise Musau),
   17 (Paul Chiasson), 80 (Dave Francis),
   81 (Ed Reinke)
Bruce Coleman Collection: 3 (center), 9,
   48, 89
Michael Gunther / Still Pictures: 50
Norman Hardy: 56
HMV Singapore Pte Ltd: 72
Fred Hoogervorst / Panos Pictures: 51
Dave G. Houser: 43, 79
The Hutchison Library: 1, 2, 3 (bottom), 5,
   8, 13, 19, 20, 21, 26, 35, 39, 42, 44, 45,
   46, 47, 49, 55, 62, 63, 64, 65, 73
Björn Klingwall: 4, 27, 87
Jason Lauré: 57
Charles D. Miller III: 36
North Wind Picture Archives: 10, 58
Betty Press / Panos Pictures: 28, 53
Marc Schlossman / Panos Pictures: 25,
   33, 54
Topham Picturepoint: 12, 40 (both), 52, 59
   (right), 66, 70, 71
Trip Photographic Library: 3 (top), 6, 18, 22,
   23, 24, 31, 32, 34, 41, 59 (left), 74, 91
University of Pennsylvania Museum
   (neg. T35-1403c & T35-1384): 60, 61
Jack Vartoogian: 85
Vision Photo Agency/Hulton Getty: 67, 76

Digital Scanning by Superskill Graphics Pte Ltd

Written by
NINA KUSHNER

Edited by
KATHARINE BROWN

Designed by
JAILANI BASARI

Picture research by
SUSAN JANE MANUEL

First published in North America in 2001 by
Gareth Stevens Publishing
A World Almanac Education Group Company
330 West Olive Street, Suite 100
Milwaukee, Wisconsin 53212 USA

For a free color catalog describing
Gareth Stevens' list of high-quality books
and multimedia programs, call
1-800-542-2595 (USA) or
1-800-461-9120 (CANADA).
Gareth Stevens Publishing's
Fax: (414) 332-3567.

© **TIMES MEDIA PRIVATE LIMITED 2001**
Originated and designed by
Times Editions
An imprint of Times Media Private Limited
A member of the Times Publishing Group
Times Centre, 1 New Industrial Road
Singapore 536196
http://www.timesone.com.sg/te

Library of Congress Cataloging-in-Publication Data
available upon request from the publisher.
Fax: (414) 336-0157 for the attention of the
Publishing Records Department.

ISBN 0-8368-2330-3

Printed in Malaysia

1 2 3 4 5 6 7 8 9 05 04 03 02 01

Contents

AN OVERVIEW OF THE DEMOCRATIC REPUBLIC OF THE CONGO

The Democratic Republic of the Congo is one of the most culturally and geographically diverse countries on Earth. The country's breathtaking landscape is the source of its wealth.

The country was known as Zaire until 1997. Today, people commonly refer to it as Congo-Kinshasa. Kinshasa is its capital city. Except where territories during Belgian rule are discussed, this text uses the official Congolese names of all territories, with their former Belgian names in parentheses at the first mention.

Opposite: **A colorfully dressed Tutsi musician and dancer perform a lion dance in Rwindi, Nord-Kivu. Their headdresses symbolize a lion's mane.**

Below: **These young children are having fun playing with Ping-Pong paddles and balls.**

THE FLAG OF THE DEMOCRATIC REPUBLIC OF THE CONGO

The Congolese flag is blue with six yellow stars running down the left side of the flag and one yellow star in the middle. The new flag was adopted on May 17, 1997, when President Mobutu Sese Seko fled the country, and rebel leader Laurent Kabila declared himself president and changed the country's name back to the Democratic Republic of the Congo. Kabila chose to use the 1960 flag as a symbolic continuation of September 1960, when Prime Minister Patrice Lumumba, his hero, was ousted from office.

Geography

The Land

Located along the equator, Congo-Kinshasa lies in the heart of Africa. It borders the Atlantic Ocean for 25 miles (40 kilometers) and shares borders with nine other countries: Angola, the Republic of the Congo, the Central African Republic, Sudan, Uganda, Rwanda, Burundi, Tanzania, and Zambia. With an area of 905,564 square miles (2,345,410 square km), Congo-Kinshasa is the third largest country in Africa, following Sudan and Algeria.

One of the most prominent features of Congo-Kinshasa is the Congo River. This river was known as the Zaire River between 1971 and 1997, when the country adopted the name Zaire. *Zaire* comes from the word *nzari* (in-ZAH-ree), which means "river." The river's course starts in the Katanga plateau and flows north, crossing the equator twice in a great arc before emptying into the Atlantic Ocean. The river is extremely important to both the history and economy of Congo-Kinshasa.

THE CONGO RIVER

The Congo ranks with the Amazon, the Nile, and the Mississippi as one of the world's longest rivers.
(*A Closer Look, page 46*)

Below: **Lush green vegetation covers the whole of Congo-Kinshasa, but only 3 percent of the country's land is under cultivation.**

The Cuvette

Congo-Kinshasa has a diverse geography. About one-third of the country is a vast basin called the Congo Basin, or *cuvette* (coo-VET), meaning "saucer" or "shallow bowl." This basin is fairly flat and low in elevation and is covered with a thick, lush tropical rain forest. Rain falls in this part of the country throughout the year. Its climate, dense forest, and marshy land make building and maintaining roads difficult.

The Ubangi-Uele plateaus in the north and the Katanga plateau in the south border the cuvette. These plateaus consist of wide savannas, grasslands, and forests.

Mountains border the cuvette to the west and east. The western Crystal Mountains stretch along the Atlantic Coast and through the Republic of the Congo. Three major mountain ranges run along Congo-Kinshasa's eastern border. They form part of the East African Rift System, an ancient geological fault. Running south to north, these ranges are the Mitumba Mountains, the volcanic Virunga Mountains, and the Ruwenzori Range (along the Ugandan border). Congo-Kinshasa's highest point is Margherita Peak on Mount Ngaliema (formerly Mount Stanley). It reaches 16,795 feet (5,119 m) and is located in the Ruwenzori Range. Mount Ngaliema is Africa's third highest mountain.

THE ITURI FOREST

Many plant, animal, and bird species are endemic to the Ituri Forest, a luxuriant rain forest in northeastern Congo-Kinshasa.
(A Closer Look, page 50)

Above: **A small village on the slopes of the Virunga Mountains, north of Lake Kivu, reaps the profits of growing corn on rich volcanic soil.**

The Climate

Although it lies along the equator, Congo-Kinshasa is not one of Africa's hottest countries. It actually has four climatic regions. In the cuvette, temperatures rarely drop below 75° Fahrenheit (24° Celsius) all year round, with high humidity and virtually no seasonal variation. Rain falls more or less continuously, averaging about 71 inches (180 centimeters) per year.

In the northern and southern plateaus, temperatures are generally cooler. These regions experience distinct wet and dry seasons. Since the two regions are on opposite sides of the equator, their seasons are also opposite. In the north, the dry season usually lasts from April to October, depending on the distance from the equator. Little or no rain falls during this period. During the same months, the south experiences its rainy season. In April, when the dry season begins in the south, it starts to rain in the north.

The cold Benguela Current and the area's low altitude affect the western coast of the country. The average temperature in Banana is 77° F (25° C), and rainfall averages 30 inches (76 cm) per year. The eastern high plateaus and mountains have an average annual temperature of 66° F (19° C), while annual rainfall is 52 inches (132 cm).

ANIMALS UNIQUE TO THE CONGO

The okapi is the national animal of Congo-Kinshasa. The Congo peacock was discovered in 1937 and is perhaps the most famous inhabitant of the Ituri Forest.

Plants and Animals

Some of Congo-Kinshasa's most spectacular plant life is found in the cuvette, where a vast intricate forest system, known as the equatorial rain forest, exists. Mahogany, ebony, rubber, and palm trees are found in this rain forest, as are many plants used to make medicine. One such plant is cinchona, which is a source of quinine, a drug used to fight the disease malaria.

Animal life is also rich and varied. Short elephants, okapis, and chimpanzees are found in the rain forest. Gorillas live in the eastern mountains. Lions and leopards roam the grasslands, while buffaloes, antelopes, jackals, hyenas, wildcats, and black and white rhinoceroses inhabit the grasslands and savannas.

Crocodiles and hippopotamuses live in and around the rivers throughout the country. Reptiles are also common and include snakes, lizards, chameleons, and turtles.

Due to hunting, many of these animal populations have decreased in recent decades. Hunting is now strictly regulated.

GORILLAS

The mountain gorilla, the most famous member of the gorilla family, is on the list of the top ten most endangered animal species in the world. (*A Closer Look, page 48*)

Left: Giraffes mainly inhabit the north-eastern grasslands of Congo-Kinshasa.

CONSERVATION

National parks set up across Congo-Kinshasa strive to conserve African wildlife. The Garamba National Park in northeastern Congo-Kinshasa is the last sanctuary for white rhinoceroses. In eastern Congo-Kinshasa, the Maiko National Park offers refuge to okapis and duikers, as well as Congo peacocks.

History

Tribal Kingdoms

The very first inhabitants of Congo-Kinshasa are believed to have been the pygmy peoples, who are thought to have arrived in late Paleolithic times. These peoples now live in the Ituri Forest.

Between the tenth and fourteenth centuries, Bantu-speaking peoples started to move into the region. By the fifteenth century, they had established dozens of separate kingdoms. One of the most important was the Kongo kingdom on the Atlantic coast, which developed a fairly elaborate political system. The king of the Bakongo, as these Bantu-speaking peoples are called, was powerful enough to collect taxes from neighboring tribes.

The Kuba federation in Kasai-Occidental was also an important precolonial political state. It consisted of about sixteen separate tribes led by the *Bushongo* (BOO-shong-go) people.

The Arrival of the Portuguese

The Portuguese were the first Europeans to travel to the Kongo kingdom. In 1482, they sailed into the mouth of the Congo River from the Atlantic Ocean and made contact with the Kongo people. The Bakongo participated with the Portuguese in slave raids in neighboring regions, and a lucrative slave trade developed. These raids led to unrest in the region, and the Kongo kingdom was in decline by the end of the 1660s.

CHILDREN OF THE FOREST

The pygmies of the Ituri Forest are nomadic hunters and gatherers who still follow their traditional way of life.
(A Closer Look, page 44)

LÉOPOLD II AND SIR HENRY MORTON STANLEY

Henry Morton Stanley, the Welsh-born American journalist and explorer who "found" Dr. David Livingstone, traced the course of the Congo River. He also helped King Léopold II of Belgium establish the Congo Free State.
(A Closer Look, page 58)

Left: Mapmaker Juan de la Cosa's map, made in 1500, shows Africa as it was known after Portuguese navigator Vasco da Gama's expedition to India via the Cape of Good Hope around Africa's southern tip between 1497 and 1499.

The Congo Free State

The only European power interested in establishing a colony in the Congo region was the tiny country of Belgium. The Belgian king, Léopold II (r. 1865–1909), had long wanted a colony. He commissioned explorer Henry Morton Stanley to set up trading posts along the Congo River and make treaties with local tribal chiefs. Léopold's colonial ambitions helped bring about the Berlin West Africa Conference of 1884 to 1885. At the conference, Léopold was recognized as the sovereign of an area that he named the Congo Free State, later called the Republic of the Belgian Congo.

The name *Congo Free State* is misleading, as it was neither free nor a state. The colony was the personal property of Léopold. In his effort to reap as much profit from it as possible, he allowed Belgian companies to enslave the local population and force them to harvest rubber vines, which grew in the forest, as well as work on the construction of railways around unnavigable sections of the Congo River.

The Belgian government finally took the Congo Free State away from Léopold in 1908 and governed it directly, following strong international criticism of Léopold's treatment of the Congolese people.

Above: **This tribal chief (*center*) poses with his warriors in front of their assembly-hut in the Belgian Congo in the early 1920s.**

THE SCRAMBLE FOR AFRICA

The Berlin West Africa Conference is the cause of many of Congo-Kinshasa's current tribal conflicts. Held between 1884 and 1885, the conference was attended by the major European powers that divided up Central and West Africa, paying no attention to African states already in existence. The lands granted to Léopold II split up numerous kingdoms and forced together peoples who were traditional enemies.

Independence

The new nation, called the Republic of the Congo, gained independence on June 30, 1960, but it was far from ready. Belgian colonial policies had fostered suspicion rather than cooperation among the country's ethnic groups. To make matters worse, most Europeans feared a violent backlash against them and abandoned the country, leaving it without professionals and administrators.

The Congo Crisis

Within weeks of independence, tensions between tribes exploded into violence. The army rebelled, leading to Belgian military intervention. Tension between President Joseph Kasavubu and Prime Minister Patrice Lumumba brought the government to a halt, and, with Belgium's support, the mineral-rich province of Katanga led by Moise Tshombe declared itself independent.

The Congo crisis escalated onto the world stage when Lumumba appealed to the international community, especially to the Soviet Union, for assistance. On September 14, 1960, Colonel Joseph Mobutu led a coup that ousted Lumumba. Lumumba was assassinated on January 17, 1961.

PATRICE LUMUMBA AND CONGOLESE NATIONALISM

Patrice Lumumba served briefly as the first prime minister of the Republic of the Congo in 1960. He was instrumental in bringing independence to the Belgian colony but fell victim to the chaos independence created.

(*A Closer Look,* page 66)

Opposite: President Mobutu waves to crowds of supporters on the streets of Kinshasa during an official parade in the early seventies.

Zaire Under Mobutu

On November 24, 1965, Mobutu staged a second coup, overthrowing President Kasavubu, and took full control of the government. With the backing of the United States, he went on to rule the Democratic Republic of the Congo, as it was then named, for thirty-two years. Mobutu brought stability to the country in his first years as president, despite two revolts that broke out in Stanleyville (now Kisangani).

In 1977 and 1978, the Congolese National Liberation Front (FLNC), the country's main opposition movement, invaded Katanga from Angola. Since Angola was a communist stronghold in southern Africa, noncommunist Western nations rallied to Mobutu's side. He suppressed these invasions with the help of external military backing from Morocco in 1977 and France and Belgium in 1978.

Mobutu's regime was extremely repressive and corrupt. He banned all political parties except for the Popular Movement of the Revolution (MPR), which he established in 1970. He also amassed a personal fortune of at least U.S. $4 billion. In the same period, the country's economy collapsed, and its people grew poorer.

AUTHENTICITÉ

In 1971, Mobutu started *authenticité* (OH-TAUNT-tee-see-TAY), a campaign designed to promote nationalism. The country's name was changed to the Republic of Zaire, and all citizens had to replace their western names with African ones.

MOBUTU SESE SEKO

Born in 1930, Mobutu ruled the Congo for thirty-two years. He single-handedly led his country down the road to bankruptcy. In May 1997, he fled the country as rebel troops reached the outskirts of Kinshasa.

(A Closer Look, page 64)

Left: **Laurent Kabila takes the oath of office as president in the national football stadium in Kinshasa on May 29, 1997. The ceremony was attended by about 40,000 people. Kabila restored the name of the country to the Democratic Republic of the Congo. The man he ousted, Mobutu Sese Seko, went into exile and died on September 7, 1997, in Rabat, Morocco.**

Rebellion and Revolution

Mobutu began to lose his grip on power in the early 1990s. In 1991, the army had been unpaid for months, and together with citizens frustrated by the economic crisis, it began a *pillage* (pee-YAHJ). As a result, Mobutu finally agreed to share power. His most severe critic, Etienne Tshisekedi, became prime minister in 1991.

The real blow to Mobutu's regime came not from the mounting problems within the country but from problems in neighboring countries. In 1994, the genocide in Rwanda and subsequent Tutsi takeover of the government drove over one million Hutu refugees into eastern Zaire, igniting tribal tensions there. General Laurent Kabila, a longtime opponent of Mobutu, harnessed this tribal discontent. He launched a rebellion that slowly spread westward across the country. Supported by neighboring countries, the rebels met with little resistance from the Zairian army. On May 17, 1997, Kabila's troops entered Kinshasa, and Kabila declared himself president.

Within fifteen months of taking power, Kabila himself was under attack from the very forces that had helped him overthrow Mobutu. Congo-Kinshasa is now engulfed in a civil war. By May 2000, rebels, supported by Rwanda, Uganda, and Burundi, had taken over and occupied much of the eastern and northeastern parts of the country. The Lusaka Peace Agreement, signed in July 1999, has been widely disregarded by both sides.

REBELLION AND CIVIL WAR

Since Laurent Kabila took power in 1997, his rule has been plagued with external intervention and internal unrest.

(A Closer Look, page 68)

Immaculée Birhaheka (1958–)

Awarded the Martin Ennals Award for Human Rights Defenders (MEA) in April 2000, Immaculée Birhaheka is the director of the leading Congolese women's organization, Promotion and Support of Women's Initiatives (PAIF). She has worked endlessly for many years to inform Congolese women of their rights. Birhaheka has been threatened, arrested, and beaten by both rebels and Rwandan troops for speaking out against mass killings and ethnic intolerance.

Joseph Kasavubu (c. 1913–1969)

Joseph Kasavubu was the first president of the Republic of the Congo. In the 1950s, he was one of the leaders of the independence movement and headed the Alliance of the Bakongo (ABAKO). ABAKO wanted the country to be a federation, a system in which each of the ethnic groups had a great deal of power. This political dream stood in contrast to that of Patrice Lumumba, head of the rival Congolese National Movement (MNC). After the country's first election in July 1960, Kasavubu and Lumumba, president and prime minister, clashed over many important issues. Kasavubu eventually dismissed Lumumba and authorized his arrest. When the latter was murdered, Kasavubu was denounced by other leaders. Mobutu overthrew him in a bloodless coup in 1965. Kasavubu died four years later.

Joseph Kasavubu

Moise Kapenda Tshombe (1919–1969)

Moise Kapenda Tshombe was president of the province of Katanga, which seceded from the Republic of the Congo on July 11, 1960. His secession was backed by Belgium. With the help of the United Nations, Tshombe's troops were defeated in January 1963, and Katanga again became part of the Republic of the Congo. Tshombe fled to Spain. With the fear of a fast-spreading peasant uprising, Tshombe was recalled to the country as prime minister in 1964. Once the threat of rebellion was over, President Kasavubu dismissed him from office on October 13, 1965. Tshombe fled the country and died in Algiers on June 29, 1969.

Moise Kapenda Tshombe

Government and the Economy

When Mobutu seized power in 1965, he turned the Democratic Republic of the Congo into a dictatorship. He rewrote the constitution, giving himself vast powers as president. Moreover, he stripped the national legislature of all authority. Increasing political and economic unrest in 1991, however, forced Mobutu to restore the power of the legislature. It seemed that the country was on its way to becoming a democracy, but it has since taken a step backward.

Under President Laurent Kabila, Congo-Kinshasa has returned to a one-party state. Kabila appointed himself president immediately following his seizure of power in May 1997, but he promised free elections and sweeping political reform. He reneged on these promises eighteen months later, when a rebellion began to make headway. Kabila suspended all transitional institutions and indefinitely postponed elections, originally scheduled for April 1999. He then used presidential decrees to grant himself broad powers, ultimately making himself head of all three branches of government: legislative, executive, and judicial.

Left: **Congolese troops patrol the streets of Kinshasa in a tank. By May 2000, Kabila ruled Congo-Kinshasa — excluding the parts occupied by rebels — through the Congolese military. Kabila appoints the judges for the Court of Military Order — now the highest court in the land.**

Left: **New Brunswick premier Bernard Lord (*left*), President Laurent Kabila (*center*), and Québec premier Lucien Bouchard (*right*) stand at attention during the Canadian National Anthem at the opening session of the VIIIe Sommet de la Francophonie (Eighth World Francophone Summit) in Moncton, New Brunswick, on September 3, 1999. At the conference, participating countries agreed to focus on human rights and youth issues, as well as on democracy. Kabila, however, has indefinitely suspended elections in Congo-Kinshasa.**

Administration

Congo-Kinshasa has ten regions: Bandundu, Bas-Congo, Équateur, Kasai-Occidental, Kasai-Oriental, Katanga, Maniema, Nord-Kivu, Orientale, and Sud-Kivu. Kinshasa, the country's capital, has a special administrative status. Each region is governed by a commissioner who is appointed by the president. The regions and Kinshasa are under the control of the highly centralized national government. According to the provisional 1998 constitution, which has since been suspended, the government of Congo-Kinshasa is a republic in which both the president and the legislature are popularly elected. Everyone over the age of eighteen can vote.

Local Life Remains the Same

Although Congo-Kinshasa has a new president, political life at the village level has not changed. Every village has a chief. This chief is usually a man and is either chosen by the villagers or has inherited his position. His main duties are to settle disputes and ensure the well-being of his people. Occasionally, a chief is not the village ruler but merely a representative of a council of elders, who are the heads of each lineage in the village. The council rules the village together, solving all important problems through debate and discussion.

Boom and Decline

When Mobutu took power, the economy was largely based on the export of copper mined in Shaba (now Katanga). In 1974, the price of copper plummeted worldwide, and Zaire's economy collapsed. By the 1980s, Zaire had incurred the largest debt for its size in the world. Today, the country's debt stands at U.S. $15 billion.

The economy took another nosedive in the 1990s, an event made worse by the pillage of 1991. Today, as a result of the foreign-backed civil war, the economy is at a standstill. Major mining and food-producing areas are occupied by the rebels, resulting in reduced exports. Many Congolese are seriously malnourished because they cannot afford to buy the food they need.

Mining

Congo-Kinshasa's main economic resource is its extensive mineral wealth, which includes large diamond, copper, cobalt, zinc, silver, gold, and platinum deposits. Before the civil war, mining accounted for 80 percent of the nation's exports. The most important mining company is the state-owned Générale des Carrières et des Mines (Gécamines). Today, most mining activities have been disrupted by the fighting.

Above: **This woman is harvesting potatoes on the volcanic slopes of the Virunga Mountains, north of Lake Kivu.**

MINING

Until the 1990s, mining supplied Congo-Kinshasa with at least three-fourths of its export earnings and was the main source of foreign currency. Due to political corruption and mismanagement, civil disturbances, and the withdrawal of international aid, modern mining operations collapsed in the early 1990s, depriving the country of most of its foreign currency earnings.
(A Closer Look, page 62)

Agriculture

Sixty-five percent of the people in Congo-Kinshasa are farmers. Before the country's independence from Belgium, farmers grew crops for export. Since its independence, however, the deterioration of the transportation networks has made it difficult for farmers to take their crops to market. This inability to transport crops has led to an increase in subsistence agriculture, where farmers grow food only for themselves or for local markets. Farm products include cassava, sweet potatoes, peanuts, and vegetables.

Most subsistence farmers use primitive, traditional farming methods that are not highly productive. Consequently, domestic food production is insufficient to meet the country's needs. Some of the foods central to the Congolese diet, such as cereals and fish, are being imported in increasing amounts.

The country's main export trading partners are Benelux (Belgium–Netherlands–Luxembourg), South Africa, and the United States. Imports come mainly from South Africa, Benelux, and China.

Transportation

Mountains, rain forests, and long rainy seasons have always made transportation difficult in Congo-Kinshasa. The lack of a good transportation network is the main reason why the country remains economically underdeveloped.

HYDROELECTRICITY

The many rapids on the Congo River provide a potential for hydroelectricity, the generation of electricity from waterpower. A massive dam at Inga Falls has the capacity to supply 2,300,000 kilowatts. The country's hydroelectric resources have an estimated potential of 13 percent of the world's capacity and 50 percent of Africa's capacity. Congo-Kinshasa currently exports electricity to neighboring nations, including Zambia, Burundi, the Republic of the Congo, and Angola.

Left: Passengers wait to board this train to Kisangani. The most important internal railway links include Lubumbashi to Ilebo, Ubundu to Kisangani, and Kinshasa to Matadi. No single railroad, however, runs the full length of the country.

RIVERBOATS

Also referred to as a "floating city," the riverboat is the main means of transportation for Congolese and tourists.
(A Closer Look, page 70)

People and Lifestyle

Ethnic Diversity

The people of Congo-Kinshasa come from over two hundred different ethnic groups, each with its own language, culture, and traditions. The three largest groups, the Mongo, the Luba, and the Kongo, are culturally and genetically related to one another. They are all part of the Bantu ethnic group that dominates much of central and southern Africa. The fourth largest group is the

KINSHASA

The wealthy and the poor live side by side in Kinshasa, making it a city of startling contrasts.
(*A Closer Look, page 54*)

Mangbetu-Azande, who live in the northeast, along the border with Sudan. They are considered Sudanic, or Hamitic, peoples. Together, these four ethnic groups make up about 45 percent of the country's population. Other large groups include the Pende, Songe, and Kuba peoples.

Since the country's independence from Belgium, a growing sense of national identity has been instilled in the Congolese, but most people still tend to identify themselves by their ethnic group first. Tragically, the current civil war has led to fighting between various ethnic groups within Congo-Kinshasa, as these groups support opposing political factions.

Above: **Life in rural Congolese villages is extremely basic. People use kerosene lamps, as villages do not have electricity, and women haul water from nearby springs, rivers, or common wells.**

City Life and Country Life: The Great Divide

Four and a half million people live in Kinshasa, the country's largest city. Great economic diversity is prevalent within the city. Those in power have tremendous wealth. Meanwhile, most *Kinois* (KEEN-wah), as the residents are called, live in poverty. With spiraling inflation and two civil wars, conditions in the city have deteriorated. Yet even in the face of such terrible economic circumstances, the Kinois, in general, are more sophisticated than their country relations; they dress in Western clothing and keep track of world affairs.

Below: **The Azande live in northern Congo-Kinshasa. In colonial times, efforts were made to relocate them into European-designed villages. Nevertheless, many still live in close-knit village communities.**

Sixty-two percent of Congolese live in villages in rural areas. Most of these people are very poor, and the civil wars have made conditions even more desperate. Hundreds of thousands of Congolese have been uprooted, and many others have had their homes and crops destroyed. Trade has been halted in most parts of the country. People suffer from malnutrition, even in areas relatively unaffected by the current civil war.

Many Congolese live in mud huts that are either square or round, with roofs made out of thatch, grass, or palm leaves. These houses are very practical. They are cool in the tropical heat, easy to build, and last at least ten years before needing repairs.

Family Life

Congolese families tend to be large, and parents may have as many as ten children. Parents invest what they can in their children, and, in return, children are expected to look after their parents when they reach old age. In recent years, the number of children per family has been shrinking, especially in urban areas where the high costs of establishing households prevent young couples from marrying at an early age.

In rural areas, Congolese families usually live in villages with members of the same ethnic group, who are often related. Extended families are also common. This means that family members outside the nuclear family often live with the family.

In most ethnic groups, a man is allowed to have more than one wife. This practice is called polygamy. The first wife usually has the most say over how the household is managed. Normally, each wife and her children have their own hut.

Since most families live without electricity or running water, they have a tremendous amount of work to do, including farming, washing the clothes, cooking, fetching water, and pounding cassava into flour.

Above: **Rural Congolese stand outside their hut near Beni in eastern Congo-Kinshasa.**

Women: The Pillars of Society

In traditional Congolese societies, men have almost all the power, but women do all the work. Congolese women work in the fields, pound cassava into flour, and wash their family's clothes by hand with water they have drawn from a well. Any money they earn outside the home is used to support the family. Currently, as the economy continues to deteriorate, the labor burdens of women in rural areas are generally increasing.

The country's independence and modernization have done little to help the status of women. Families still generally choose to educate their sons over their daughters, resulting in a higher literacy rate for men (about 86.6 percent) than for women (about 67.7 percent). Married women need their husband's permission to open a bank account or obtain a commercial license.

Despite cultural and legal constraints, urban women have made some progress in the professional world. Since the 1990s, a growing number of women have been working in professional occupations in areas such as government services, the military, and the universities. Yet few of these women have high-level jobs, and they usually earn less than their male counterparts.

THE FAMILY CODE

In 1987, Mobutu passed the Family Code, a law that legalized polygamy. It also allowed a husband to legally claim his wife's property without having the responsibility of supporting her or their children. Congolese women had hoped that Laurent Kabila would repeal the Family Code, but so far no action has been taken.

Left: **Rural Congolese women are saddled with the bulk of agricultural work, firewood gathering, water collection and hauling, and child care.**

Education

Today, at 77.3 percent, Congo-Kinshasa has one of the highest literacy rates in all of Africa. This success, however, is due largely to the work of missionaries, who teach over half the nation's students. Even at the best of times, state schools suffer from extreme shortages, ranging in anything from chalk to teachers. In times of economic hardship, the government often closes schools.

Another problem is that parents frequently do not send their children to school because it simply costs too much, or they need their children's help with family businesses. Students at all levels

must pay tuition fees. They must also purchase uniforms, books, and supplies.

In Congo-Kinshasa, elementary school, which includes grades one to six, is compulsory. The curriculum is set at the national level by the minister of education. It includes French, mathematics, natural science, geography, and history. In grade one, students are taught in their local language. French is gradually introduced as the language of instruction in the following grades, and, by the sixth grade, it is the only language spoken in the classroom. At the end of grade six, students take an examination to determine whether they can enter middle school.

Above: **The Congolese education system still depends mainly on missionary schools, such as this evangelistic mission high school, to provide public education.**

Middle school begins with a two-year program that evaluates students' strengths and weaknesses. The program also gives students advice and guidance on future study and career choices. If students do well in the first two years, they go on to enroll in a four-year high school program. This program includes business, education, literature, mathematics, nursing, and science courses. At the end of this program, students take the national examination, and the results determine whether they can go on to a university. If students do not do well in the middle school program, they can take a two-year course that trains them in vocational skills.

Below: **Students at a post-high school institution take a break from their studies.**

Congo-Kinshasa has three state universities, the largest being the University of Kinshasa (the former Lovanium University). The country also has at least one post-high school institution in each district. These institutes are devoted to various fields of study, including law, teacher training, nursing, business, and the arts. Kinshasa's School of Catholic Theology is known throughout the world. As public universities are usually plagued by political and social problems, the Congolese have established several privately funded and administrated universities. Many schools and universities, however, have either closed or been heavily disrupted due to the current civil war.

Religion

Congo-Kinshasa does not have an official religion, although the majority of the population practices some form of Christianity. About 50 percent of the people are Roman Catholic, and 20 percent are Protestant. Another 10 percent are Kimbanguist, followers of an African Christian church. Ten percent follow traditional beliefs, and the remaining 10 percent are Muslim. Islam entered the country in the nineteenth century with the arrival of Arab and Swahili slave and ivory traders from the East African coast.

Traditional Beliefs

Before Europeans brought Christianity to the region, the ethnic groups that today make up Congo-Kinshasa practiced their own religions. About one of every ten Congolese still practices these beliefs today. All these traditional religions have certain elements in common. One is the worship of ancestors who have moved on to the next world but still have power to influence events in

CHURCH AND STATE

Given its role in national education and religious life, the Catholic Church has the potential to challenge the power of the government. Always wary of this possibility, Mobutu worked hard to reduce the power of the Church. As part of the authenticité campaigns, he banned all religious radio and television shows. He also set himself up as a demigod. The state-controlled media referred to him as "the Guide, the father of the Nation," sent by God to lead the country.

this one. Another element is the worship, or at least the recognition, of spirits that inhabit the natural world, such as tree spirits, water spirits, and spirits that control the harvest, the rains, and the clouds.

Africanized Christianity

Initially, Christianity in Congo-Kinshasa was modeled after religious practices in the West. Today, however, most Christian churches in the country have been Africanized, meaning that local culture has greatly influenced church services. The Catholic Church in Congo-Kinshasa is now led by Congolese bishops, and church services are conducted in local languages with hymns sung to local melodies and rhythms. Protestant churches have also experienced Africanization.

In some cases, African roots and Christian traditions have combined to form new, breakaway African churches. The largest of these is the Kimbanguist church, founded by Simon Kimbangu, a religious leader who rejected magic, polygamy, and other elements of traditional religion. A second, more radical group is the Kitawalas. Originally part of the Watch Tower Bible and Tract Society (Jehovah's Witnesses), the Kitawalas broke away and formed their own church. They believe in the existence of a black god, and they denounce all other forms of authority.

Opposite: **A procession of Catholic worshipers waits to attend Mass at a church in Kimpese.**

KIMBANGUISM

Simon Kimbangu's separatist church, which was founded in 1921, transcends class, tribal, and national boundaries. Prior to Congolese independence, his church was a center of resistance against Belgian colonial rule.
(A Closer Look, page 52)

Left: **This mosque is located in the city of Butembo. Today, Congolese Muslims live primarily in the eastern part of the country, where they remain quite isolated. They still wear the long white robes that were characteristic of their Middle Eastern ancestors.**

Language and Literature

More than two hundred languages and dialects are spoken in Congo-Kinshasa, all of which originate from the Bantu language family. Four of these languages have become the national languages of the country: Lingala, Swahili (or Kiswahili), Tshiluba, and Kikongo. Lingala is the most common language spoken in Kinshasa, and it is also used by the military. Swahili is the lingua franca of the east and northeast; Tshiluba is spoken more in the south and central areas; and Kikongo is spoken in the area between Kinshasa and the coast. French, however, is the official language of Congo-Kinshasa. It is the language of instruction in all schools and is used in government.

An Oral Culture

Congolese cultures are known as oral cultures. Communication often takes place through speaking rather than writing. Even the collective information of an ethnic group, such as its history, is traditionally stored in people's minds.

MDUDYE

An *mdudye* (em-DUH-DEE-yay), or "man of memory," is an official of the Luba people who recites the history of the Luba kingdom. To aid him in his recitation, which can take days, he uses a *lusaka* (loo-SAH-kah). The lusaka is a flat, hand-held board covered with beads or pins. The beads represent events and people, such as certain battles and heroes.

Left: **This newspaper vendor is selling French newspapers on a street in Kinshasa.**

Congolese Literature

Congolese literature began to develop only after colonial independence in 1960. This was facilitated in 1962 by the founding of Romans d'Inspiration Africaine, or African Inspired Novels, a literature center at Lovanium University. This center educated and helped inspire and support many Congolese writers. One of the most important writers to emerge from this center is Philippe Lisembé Elebe (1937–). Themes tackled by Congolese writers include Congolese identity, colonialism, tribalism, and conflicts between modernity and tradition.

A prominent Congolese female writer is Clémentine Faik-Nzuji (1944–). Although she attended a university in Paris and today teaches in Belgium, she has written numerous books of poetry about her native land, including *Murmures*, or *Murmurs*. Published in 1967, *Murmures* is considered one of the very first works to be written and published by an African female writer in French. She won first prize for poetry in the President L. S. Senghor Literary Competition in 1969.

Women writers continue to play an important role in Congolese literature. Elisabeth Mweya Tol'ande (1947–) is well known for her contribution to French African literature and was awarded the Mobuto Seseko Prize for Poetry in 1972.

Arts

Congo-Kinshasa is world famous for its tribal art. Unlike many parts of Africa, where modernization has weakened tribal artistic traditions, dozens of the country's ethnic groups, including the Luba, Kongo, Pende, Kuba, Yaka, Songe, Lega, and Azande peoples, still continue to produce a spectacular variety of dramatic and beautiful masks, cloth, statues, and carvings.

Art in Everyday Life

Simple everyday objects, such as bowls, cups, combs, goblets, tools, knives, pots and lids, pipes, and boxes, are finely carved or decorated by the Congolese. To make a living, many Congolese artists supplement their income from the sale of their artwork with farming or other work.

Sometimes the pieces of art have special social purposes. Among the Woyo people, a woman is given a set of carved pot lids when she marries. Each lid illustrates a proverb about the relationship between a husband and wife. If the wife feels that her husband is mistreating her, she serves him a meal in a pot with the appropriate lid. She does this in front of guests. The husband is then obliged to talk through the problem with his wife, while the guests act as mediators.

Religious Art

Most Congolese works of art, especially sculptures, are not everyday objects but items used for religious purposes. Special masks and costumes are used for rituals, such as marriages, funerals, and initiations of boys into manhood. Statues are another important form of religious art. Most religious statues are made of wood. Some have human hair, fur, or raffia fibers attached to them. Fetishes are another type of religious sculpture common to most ethnic groups. They are tools used by sorcerers to perform magic, such as protecting a community from its enemies.

As so much artwork is used in magic, artists are believed to be close to the forces of magic, as well as to the souls of the dead. If they were not, the fetishes and other objects that they make would have no power. For this reason, artists are highly respected members of Congolese society.

MASKS

Congolese tribes, including the Kuba and Luba, carve masks with distinctive traditional styles that are used in age-old rituals, such as initiation ceremonies.
(*A Closer Look, page 61*)

STATUS SYMBOLS

Many commonplace objects are so beautiful that they often serve as status symbols. Every adult member of the Mbole people, a forest tribe, has a whistle that she or he wears every day. The more elaborately carved the whistle, the greater the status of its owner. This is because only the wealthy or the powerful can afford such ornate and costly items.

KUBA CLOTH

Textiles are very important to the Kuba people. Virtually all members of its adult society are involved in the production of beautiful and intricately designed cloth.
(*A Closer Look, page 56*)

Opposite: This stool was made for a Luba chief. The so-called "long-face style" is one of the main styles of the Luba-Henda people.

Above: **Congolese children make music, playing bright yellow brass instruments.**

Music and Dance

Music is a vital part of Congolese life, both in the countryside and in the city. Common instruments are rattles, bells, wooden xylophones, horns, traditional stringed instruments, drums, and flutes made of wood, bamboo, or reeds. The *kalimba* (kah-LIM-bah), or lamellaphone, is also very popular. It is a wooden board with thin metal strips nailed to it. Although it looks like a piano, musicians pluck the "keys" rather than pound them.

In Congo-Kinshasa, music and dance play a central role in traditional religious rituals. Each ritual has its own music and dance. For example, a Kuba ritual for paying respect to ancestors requires participants not only to wear particular costumes and masks but also to dance a specially choreographed dance to certain melodies and rhythms.

Dance is also an important educational tool. Repetitive dances teach children physical control and emphasize accepted standards of conduct. Sometimes children form their own dance groups or join adults at the end of the dance line.

Dance and music are two of the main forms of entertainment all over the country. Congolese bands have excelled in the creation of their own popular dance music called *Soukous* (SOO-koos), or African rumba. Soukous has gained popularity all over Africa and increasingly in Europe and North America. It is not possible to enter any bar or restaurant in Congo-Kinshasa without hearing it on the radio. In the bigger towns, Soukous bands play live in nightclubs while patrons dance.

Left: **Dance is very important to the Congolese people. Here, two women unwind and dance the night away at a nightclub in Kisangani.**

SOUKOUS

Known to his adoring fans as "the sorcerer of the guitar," Franco Luambo was one of the most influential Soukous musicians of all times.
(A Closer Look, page 72)

Leisure and Festivals

Children's Games

The toys of most Congolese children are objects that they have made. Children use bamboo, old tin cans, discarded boxes, and worn-out tires to construct miniature toy trucks with wheels, fake glasses, wagons, and even little motorcycles. Boys are more likely than girls to spend long hours playing with these objects. Girls generally play by imitating their mothers at work. As a mother walks with her baby tied to her back, her small daughter may walk beside her with a doll tied to hers. The games are good training because girls are put to work at a very early age, even as young as four or five years old. Young girls are usually put in charge of their younger siblings. A young girl is often seen with an infant tied to her back.

Urban and Rural Pastimes

Singing and dancing are the main forms of entertainment for most Congolese. In rural areas, wealthier villagers may hire drummers to celebrate an important occasion, such as the homecoming of a son working abroad, the birth of a child, or a good harvest. Both men and women dance, although usually not together.

Below: **The Congolese are very inventive and can make virtually anything out of basic materials. Here, young children proudly show off their wooden homemade scooters.**

Above: **This disc jockey works hard to entertain patrons at a nightclub in Kinshasa.**

In cities, residents enjoy a wider variety of pastimes. People who own televisions love to watch television dramas. Movies, which can be seen in most towns, are also popular. Some Congolese spend their leisure time playing cards.

In Kinshasa, open-air bars and nightclubs provide nightlife for urban Congolese. These places offer people the chance to unwind and dance to the lively music of Soukous bands.

Families in Congo-Kinshasa do not take vacations together as many do in the West. Instead, children are often sent to stay with relatives in a distant province or even abroad for a few months. Once there, the children may continue to perform the same chores that they do at home, such as helping with the farm work or household chores.

Storytelling

Storytelling, an ancient form of entertainment in almost every oral culture, is of particular importance to the Congolese. Traditionally, the village storyteller recounts a folk tale that contains a moral. A modern form of storytelling has emerged more recently in the bars and cafés of the big cities; news and stories are told about people in the public eye, such as politicians or actors.

Mankala

Mankala (man-KAH-lah) is an ancient African game that is popular in West African countries, as well as in Congo-Kinshasa. It is played on a rectangular board or playing area with fourteen pits, which are usually holes scooped out of the ground. Each side of the board has a strip of six round pits and a long or rounded pit called a treasury at each end. Each player controls one of the strips of six round pits and one of the treasuries. The playing pieces are stones, seeds, shells, or beans. The object of the game is to "capture" all the opponent's stones.

The game begins by distributing four stones into each of the pits. The first player takes all the stones from any of his or her pits and drops them one at a time into the neighboring pits, moving counterclockwise. The moving player drops a stone into his or her treasury if he or she passes it but not into the opponent's treasury. If the last stone is dropped into the moving player's treasury, he or she gets another turn.

If the last stone falls into an empty pit on the player's side, he or she can "capture" the opponent's stones in the pit directly opposite. The captured stones are stored in the moving player's treasury. After a capture, it is the opponent's turn.

The game ends when all the pits on one side are empty. The player who still has stones in any of his or her pits is allowed to put them all into the treasury. The winner is the player with the most stones.

THE ORIGINS OF MANKALA

Variations of mankala are played not only in Africa but in many countries around the world. The Congolese, however, claim it as their own. They believe that the game was invented by King Shamba Bolongongo (c. 1600), the ninety-third king of the Bakuba, in order to lure his people away from gambling.

Sports

Soccer is the national sport of Congo-Kinshasa and is played at all levels. Boys play it throughout the dry season, often using a bunch of rags as a ball. Many villages have both youth and adult teams. The Simbas are the country's national team.

Basketball has been popular, especially in Kinshasa and Lubumbashi, since the 1960s and is played in schools around the country. All three of Congo-Kinshasa's state universities have basketball teams. The Congolese also enjoy other sports, such as boxing, swimming, and riverboat racing.

THE SUCCESS OF THE SIMBAS

The Simbas, formerly named the Leopards during Mobutu's rule, qualified for the World Cup in 1974 and won the African Nations Cup that same year. In July 2000, Fédération Internationale de Football Association (FIFA), the world body governing soccer, ranked the Congolese soccer team seventieth in the world.

Left: Burkina Faso's Talle Ibrahima (*left*) fights for the ball with Congo-Kinshasa's Tondelua Mbuilua (*right*) during the third-place final of the African Nations Cup in Ouagadougou, Burkina Faso, on February 27, 1998. Congo-Kinshasa beat Burkina Faso 4-1.

Official Holidays

The difficult political and economic climate in Congo-Kinshasa has dampened popular celebrations of secular holidays. Official holidays have always been used by the government to drum up patriotism and celebrate the regime. Kabila, like Mobutu before him, marks these days with large military displays, especially parades, intended to show the nation and the world the country's defense capability.

The most important state holiday is Independence Day, held on June 30. Independence Day celebrates the country's break with Belgium in 1960 and its establishment as an independent country.

PARENTS' DAY

Parents' Day in Congo-Kinshasa is on August 1. The Congolese remember the dead in the morning and celebrate the living in the afternoon. Residents of Kinshasa go to the cemeteries early in the morning to clear family graves. They set fires to burn away the tall weeds and elephant grass that have grown during the rainy season. After sweeping the graves, the adults either eat a meal at the site or have a drink for good health and protection from spirits. They then go home and eat a meal with their children.

Left: Colorful and lavish celebrations are held throughout Congo-Kinshasa every year on June 30 to celebrate Independence Day.

Traditional Festivals

Traditional festivals in Congo-Kinshasa are of several varieties. Some involve worshiping ancestors or spirits. Others center around major events in an individual's life, such as birth, initiation, or marriage. Initiation, one of the most important events, marks a child's passage into adulthood. For a boy in the Bambuti (BAM-BOOT-ee) tribes of the Ituri Forest, initiation is characterized by a long period of training in which he learns the things he will need to know as a man. This sacred knowledge may include religious instruction or hunting skills. The boy is often put through various physical trials to prove he is up to the task of being an adult in his community. At the end, the ritual of circumcision marks his new status as a man. When the ritual is complete, the village has a huge party to celebrate.

Christian Holidays

Christian holy days are public holidays in Congo-Kinshasa. These days include Easter Monday, Ascension Day, Whitmonday, and Christmas Day.

Above: **Initiation dances are very important to the Bapende tribe, which lives in western and central Congo-Kinshasa. The dances mark a boy's transition from child to adult.**

Food

With its geographic and ethnic diversity, Congo-Kinshasa has a wide variety of foods and delicacies. Although the Congolese have been known to eat elephant, deer, monkey, and wild lizard, their more standard sources of protein are chicken and fish. *Moambé* (MOW-am-bay) is the national dish. It is prepared by cooking chicken in a spicy sauce made with peanut butter, tomatoes, ginger, oil, and pepper. Monkey stew is also a big favorite of the Congolese. Meat is generally purchased at weekly markets, but it is so expensive that an average villager will eat it only once a week, if that.

Above: **A boy proudly shows off fish that he has caught. Fish is a common part of the Congolese diet.**

Left: **This woman is pounding cassava into a powder. The powder is mixed with water and then cooked for several minutes.**

40

Left: **This mealie meal has been prepared for lunch for participants of a church convention in Kinshasa. Mealie meal is a cornmeal porridge made by mixing cornmeal with water. The mixture is then stirred until it becomes a semisolid.**

Most food in the Congolese diet, however, is not purchased but grown. The basis of most meals is some kind of starch, either rice, manioc bread, or cassava, a root that is pounded into flour and made into a dough-like substance. The rice, manioc bread, or cassava is always served with a sauce. Congolese prefer hot, spicy sauces, although many are made with manioc greens, leaves from local trees, or peanut butter. The sauce usually contains vegetables and sometimes meat or fish. Special occasions often call for foods made with a lot of palm oil, which is prepared locally. A wide variety of fruits is also readily available.

Dining Etiquette

The midday meal is the main meal of the day. This meal is usually served in a large common bowl, which is sometimes placed on the ground, often on a mat. After washing their hands, family members squat around the bowl and begin to eat. Everyone eats with one hand, usually the right. Each person takes a handful of rice, manioc bread, or cassava and combines it with the sauce in the bowl to make a ball. The ball of food is then eaten. Doing this neatly is much harder than it looks.

When they can, the Congolese cook more than they can eat because visitors could always drop in. It is considered very rude in Congolese society not to offer or not to accept food and drink.

GRASSHOPPER POPCORN

In Congo-Kinshasa, certain insects, such as locusts, termites, and ants, are considered great delicacies. They are eaten raw, roasted, or fried. In addition to being quite tasty, insects are a good source of protein.

MALNUTRITION

Declining economic circumstances, brought on by escalating inflation and civil wars, have decreased the food supply in Congo-Kinshasa and caused widespread malnutrition. A further tragedy is that generations of Congolese have been growing up undernourished on a basic diet of cassava, which has very low nutritional value.

A CLOSER LOOK AT THE DEMOCRATIC REPUBLIC OF THE CONGO

Too often, Congo-Kinshasa is associated with dictators and political repression. Although the country's history has been characterized by mismanagement and a lack of freedom, the political life of the nation is not the only factor that influences the everyday lives of its citizens. The environment is equally important. The country's tropical rain forests, wide savannas, and rugged mountains are home to hundreds of species of animals and plants, many of which are endangered.

Congo-Kinshasa also remains a country rich in artistic tradition. From traditional masks and cloth made in tiny villages all over the country to the electrified sound of Soukous blasting out of speakers in a Kinshasa nightclub, Congo-Kinshasa's arts celebrate life.

Opposite: **Tourists take a close look at the souvenirs locals are selling on the main street of Bukavu.**

Left: **These young Congolese women strike a pose at a window of a building in Kinshasa.**

Children of the Forest

Pygmies were the first inhabitants of Congo-Kinshasa. Collectively known as the Bambuti, the *Mbuti* (em-BOOT-ee), *Efe* (AY-fay), *Aka* (AH-kah), and *Sua* (soo-WAH) pygmies live much as they did one thousand years ago as nomadic hunter-gatherers in the Ituri Forest. They are culturally and genetically different from their Bantu neighbors. Their skin is lighter in color, they differ in blood type, and they are famously short. On average, a man measures less than 4 feet 6 inches (1.37 m) in height.

Below: **Most pygmy groups are slowly being influenced by the outside world. More and more of them are starting to wear Western-style clothes in place of their traditional attire.**

The Mbuti pygmies call themselves *bamiki bandura* (bah-MEEK-ee bon-DURE-ah), which means "children of the forest," because they rely on the forest for their survival. They hunt elephants, duikers, and other game for meat, which they eat or trade. The Mbuti also gather mushrooms, honey, and fruits. They live in beehive-shaped huts covered with leaves, and they fashion their clothes from the inner bark of certain trees. Mbuti religion involves the worship of the forest. The Mbuti believe that their ancestors were born from trees. Most Mbuti artwork, from their painted bark-cloth clothing to their songs and dances, involves some sort of celebration of *ndura* (in-DURE-ah), or forestness.

Cultural Values: Community and Play

Community is very important to the Mbuti. They have no chiefs. Instead, they solve problems through group discussion. These nomadic people travel in bands of ten to twenty-five families, stopping for a month at a time in an area that seems particularly rich in game. Children are often passed from family to family so that they get to know the entire band. They also call all adults "mother" and "father."

Although there is an emphasis on community, the Mbuti divide labor according to gender. Men are responsible for hunting. They use large nets woven from bark gathered by the

RELATIONSHIPS OF DEPENDENCE

The Mbuti associate with the Bila (BEE-lah), an agricultural Bantu tribe that lives near the forest. The Mbuti swap meat, honey, medicine, and labor for crops such as tobacco, manioc, rice, and peanuts. The Bila are dependent on the Mbuti for their help in the fields.

women. They also make bark cloth by hammering pieces of the fibrous plant tissue with wooden mallets. Women are in charge of food gathering and domestic work, such as cooking. They also dye the bark cloth prepared by the men and sew the pieces into clothing. Women have a say in the band's decisions, but their opinions do not carry as much weight as the men's do.

For Mbuti children, play is an extremely important activity. Children's games teach the children to be social, to depend on each other, and to work together to solve problems. The Mbuti are fond of joke telling and imitations. They are known to begin to sing or dance spontaneously, usually at night.

Above: **Mbuti men look on as the women prepare the community's meal from roots and vegetables they have gathered.**

The Congo River

With a length of about 2,900 miles (4,667 km), the Congo River is the second longest river in Africa, after the Nile. The Congo drains water from an area of some 1,335,000 square miles (3,457,650 square km). This drainage basin covers not only the entire country, but most of the Republic of the Congo, the Central African Republic, eastern Zambia, northern Angola, and parts of Tanzania and Cameroon as well. The Congo River dumps about 1,450,000 cubic feet (41,000 cubic meters) of water into the Atlantic

Below: **Many rural Congolese settle in small villages along the banks of the Congo River.**

Ocean every second. Such quantities of water make the Congo the second largest river in the world in terms of volume. The Amazon River is the largest. The river is 10 miles (16 km) wide in some places, and it contains over four thousand islands.

A Curving Course

The Lualaba River officially becomes the Congo River just west of Kisangani. From there, its course takes the form of a great arc. The river flows to the northwest, west, and finally southwest before passing through Congo-Kinshasa's capital and draining into the Atlantic Ocean at Banana.

A MYSTERY UNRAVELED

The course of the Congo River was a great mystery until the late nineteenth century, when British explorer Henry Morton Stanley followed its path across the African continent. He discovered that the Lualaba River was the source of the Congo River.

Sailing the Congo

Within Congo-Kinshasa, the Congo River and its tributaries make up 8,700 miles (14,000 km) of navigable rivers. It is the greatest network of usable waterways on the African continent. Water travel is increasingly important in Congo-Kinshasa, as other means of transportation, such as roads, lie in disrepair.

The Congo River itself, however, is not entirely navigable. The first obstacle, Inga (Livingstone) Falls, lies downstream from Kinshasa. A boat entering the Congo River from the Atlantic Ocean is able to sail only 84 miles (135 km) to the town of Matadi, at which point it comes face to face with the famous series of

Below: **A solitary canoeist takes in the tranquillity and beauty of the surrounding forests as he punts along the Congo River.**

thirty-two cataracts, or waterfalls. All river traffic stops there. People wishing to go upstream must drive or take a train around the falls. The obstacle presented by the falls is so great that it prevented large-scale exploration of the inland region for centuries. Exploration became possible only when Stanley built a railroad around the cataracts in the late nineteenth century.

It is smooth sailing from Kinshasa to Kisangani, a distance of over 1,000 miles (1,600 km). Just south (upstream) of Kisangani is the second obstacle, Boyoma (Stanley) Falls. Again, all river traffic stops. Travelers and cargo must continue overland around the falls before setting sail again on the Congo River.

Gorillas

Gorillas are among Congo-Kinshasa's most famous wildlife. With a huge, powerful, barrel-like chest, long arms, and short, stocky legs, an adult male can grow up to 5.5 feet (1.67 m) and weigh between 298 and 606 pounds (135 and 275 kg). The male often has gray or silver hair on the lower part of its back and is called a "silverback." The female, which is about half the size of the male, gives birth once every three to four years. She carries the baby in her arms until it is three months old, at which time it travels around clinging to her back. Gorillas have a life expectancy of up to thirty years.

Gorillas are social animals, living and traveling in packs, which number from six to twenty. They eat twice a day, and their diet is vegetarian. They eat mainly bamboo. They also eat berries, wild celery, and thistles. Gorillas do not need to drink because all the water they need is contained in their food.

Despite the aggressive portrayals of gorillas in movies, such as *King Kong*, these animals are actually quite shy. They become aggressive only if they feel threatened. In these instances, an adult male may beat his chest, make loud noises, or rush at the intruder.

Several types of gorillas live in Congo-Kinshasa. Lowland gorillas make their home in the lowland rain forests. Eastern

Left: **A mother mountain gorilla embraces her baby. Deforestation and human exploitation threaten the survival of these large, gentle mammals and has made them some of the rarest animals on Earth.**

lowland gorillas live in the tropical rain forests in the eastern part of the country.

The now-endangered mountain gorillas receive the most media attention. These gorillas live in the mountains in eastern Congo-Kinshasa, as well as in Rwanda and Uganda. In the past, poachers illegally trapped and killed these animals for their hands, feet, heads, and skins, which were believed to have certain magical or healing powers. Such activities drastically reduced the mountain gorilla population from somewhere between 5,000 and 15,000 in the 1960s to approximately 620 today.

The plight of the mountain gorillas became headline news mainly through the work of American primatologist Dian Fossey (1932–1985), the subject of the Hollywood film *Gorillas in the Mist*. She began watching gorillas in the Democratic Republic of the Congo in 1967. She then moved to Rwanda where she established the Karisoke Research Center.

Although poaching is less of a problem now than it was in the past, the mountain gorilla population is still in danger. Wars in the area have destroyed their habitat, and they have started contracting human diseases from well-meaning tourists who get too close.

Today, most of the country's magnificent mountain gorillas live in the 3,012-square-mile (7,801-square-km) Virunga National Park. Founded in 1925 as a wildlife refuge, the park contains some of the most dramatic landscapes in Africa.

Above: **In addition to the endangered mountain gorilla, the Virunga National Park shelters okapis, wild dogs, chimpanzees, colobus monkeys, and aardvarks.**

The Ituri Forest

The rain forests of Congo-Kinshasa cover two-fifths of the country, mainly in the north and east. The northeastern Ituri Forest is of particular importance because it is home to plants and animals found nowhere else on Earth. Named after the Ituri River, which runs through it, the forest remains one of the least-known regions on Earth. Scientists estimate its area to be approximately 24,300 square miles (62,900 square km).

Layers of Life

The Ituri Forest is an equatorial, or tropical, rain forest. Vertical layers of life characterize this type of forest. At the very top is the emergent layer, made up of trees that reach up to 170 feet (52 m) in height. Their trunks are sometimes 4 feet (1.2 m) in diameter. These trees, however, are not very common. There are usually only one or two of them per acre (0.4 hectare).

The canopy is below the emergent layer. This layer consists of the flat crowns of another series of trees that grow between 50 and 150 feet (15 and 46 m) in height. These trees are so close together that their branches and leaves intertwine, blocking most of the sunlight from the forest floor. Growing up the trunks of

Below: **The emergent and canopy layers of the Ituri Forest prevent sunlight from reaching the forest floor.**

Left: **The okapi makes its home in the Ituri Forest. It feeds on leaves and fruit.**

A DELICATE BALANCE

The equatorial rain forest has a very delicate ecosystem. To survive, each species of plant and animal has adapted itself to live in a very specific set of circumstances. Competition for nutrients in the soil, for example, has encouraged the growth of epiphytes. These are plants that attach themselves to other plants. They then take what nutrients they need from the air. Centuries of such adaptation has resulted in complete interdependence among species. If one species is wiped out, the ecosystem will become unbalanced, and many other species will be destroyed as a result.

these trees and hanging down from their branches are creepers or vines, some of which are more than 1 foot (30 cm) thick. The rubber vine is a creeper that grows naturally in the Ituri Forest. Monkeys, baboons, hundreds of species of birds, and thousands of species of insects, including many bright butterflies, live in the canopy layer.

Below the canopy, in the understory, the forest is humid and fairly dark. Rain falls frequently above the canopy. Protecting the forest floor from a direct downpour, the canopy creates a stable climate underneath. The forest is always humid and stays at a temperature of about 80° F (27° C).

Various large animals make their homes on the forest floor, most notably okapis, relatives of the giraffe. Lowland gorillas also live in the forest. They are smaller and more aggressive than their mountain cousins. Leopards, African golden cats, forest buffalo, and short elephants are also native to the area.

Kimbanguism

Simon Kimbangu was the founder of a mass religious movement that eventually grew into the largest independent Christian church in Africa. His church was the first African church to be admitted to the World Council of Churches in 1969. Today, the Kimbanguist Church is officially called the Church of Jesus Christ on Earth Through the Prophet Simon Kimbangu. The church is estimated to have from one to three million members across Central Africa, not including the numerous splinter groups that follow the message of Kimbangu but do not officially belong to the church.

Born near the town of Thysville (now Mbanza-Ngungu) in 1889, Simon Kimbangu was raised in the British Baptist Missionary Society's mission in Lower Congo (now Bas-Congo), where he became a Christian. In 1921, Kimbangu claimed that he had been called by a divine revelation to heal the sick. In April of that year, he began to tour Lower Congo and supposedly effected miraculous cures. Soon, Kimbangu added biblical messages to his sermons, and thousands flocked to hear him speak. Among the Bakongo, the people of that area, he was called *Ngunza* (in-GUN-zah), a Kikongo word meaning "prophet" or "doer of miracles."

Kimbangu's message was Christian, but he was stricter than most of the local missions. He preached against traditional

Left: **The Kimbanguist movement celebrated its forty-sixth anniversary in 1967, with a ceremony outside a Kimbanguist church in Kinshasa.**

religion and forbade magic, fetishes, and polygamy. The Belgian colonial authorities became increasingly alarmed by the disturbances that Kimbangu provoked. Despite the fact that he had no particular interest in politics himself, Kimbangu's movement soon became a center of resistance against Belgian colonial rule.

In October 1921, the colonial administrators took action. They arrested Kimbangu, tried him for insurrection, and then sentenced him to death. The sentence was later reduced to life in prison. Kimbangu spent the rest of his days in a jail cell in Élisabethville (now Lubumbashi), where he died in 1951. Followers of his movement were either deported or persecuted.

Belgian efforts to crush the Kimbanguist movement only seemed to make it more popular. Ngunzaism, as the movement was then called, not only spread throughout the country but across its borders to the Republic of the Congo and Angola. Kimbangu's message appealed to men and women of all classes, as well as many different ethnic groups.

By the 1950s, there were many different sects or groups of people following Kimbanguism. One group, based near Thysville, was led by Simon Kimbangu's youngest son, Joseph Diangienda. Diangienda founded the official Kimbanguist Church, which gained state recognition in 1959.

THE KIMBANGUIST CHURCH TODAY

Today, the Kimbanguist Church remains removed from politics. Its members lead a rather austere lifestyle. They do not partake in traditional religious practices, and they avoid alcohol, tobacco, dancing, and violence. The church does extensive missionary work in the agricultural, health, and education sectors.

Kinshasa

Kinshasa, formerly Léopoldville, is the capital of Congo-Kinshasa. The city is located 320 miles (515 km) from the Atlantic Ocean, just upriver from the famous Inga Falls. Not only is Kinshasa the center of Congo-Kinshasa's political life, it is also the center of the country's popular culture.

Shortly after the country's independence, Kinshasa received immigrants from West Africa and neighboring countries in Central Africa. Today, many Kinois are rural migrants. Political

THE CAPITAL CITY

Léopoldville, named after King Léopold II of Belgium, was founded by Henry Morton Stanley in 1881. It became the capital of the country in the late 1920s and was renamed Kinshasa in 1966.

turmoil, the economic decline of rural areas, and the attraction of city life have caused them to come to Kinshasa to find work. More often than not, they fail. Unemployment rates are high, and, consequently, so is the crime rate. The city has had enormous problems keeping up with its population growth.

One of the major problems is food. Although Kinshasa imports vegetables from as far away as South Africa, few can afford them. Many Kinois keep vegetable gardens on small plots of soil near their homes. Water supply is another problem. Most people live in concrete block houses with corrugated tin roofs, which were hastily erected to house the growing population.

Above: **Cars drive along Boulevard du 30 juin in Kinshasa. Kinshasa is the nation's main administrative, cultural, and economic center. Today, it has over 4.5 million inhabitants, making it not only the largest city in Congo-Kinshasa, but one of the largest cities in Africa.**

Most of these houses do not have running water, and, since so many of the public taps are broken, women often walk miles (km) each day to collect water. Many homes have no electricity, and those that do must contend with an erratic supply. Food is cooked over open fires. The forests around Kinshasa have all been cut down, making firewood a rare and expensive commodity.

The plight of many Kinois grew more desperate after the collapse of the economy in the early 1990s and has recently deteriorated even further because of the current civil war. By the spring of 1999, most Kinois could only afford one meal a day, and the disruption of trade had caused many businesses to close.

Below: **As most Kinois experience extreme poverty, they try to sell any worthy goods they possess on the streets throughout the capital.**

In the midst of this widespread poverty, however, is a dynamic and vibrant cultural life. At the heart of that life is the section of the city known as La Cité. Here, streets are lined with open-air bars and numerous nightclubs, as well as four casinos. La Cité is also where Soukous, the popular music style, developed.

The vibrancy of La Cité and the poverty of most of the city's other areas stand in contrast to La Gombe, the old European section of the city. Today, it is home to the Congolese elite, who live in spacious villas surrounded by beautiful gardens. Central government buildings and the embassy district are also located in this part of the capital.

Kuba Cloth

Called "People of Lightning" by their Luba neighbors, the Kuba people live in the Kasai-Occidental region of Congo-Kinshasa, between the Kasai and Sankuru rivers. They are a confederation of about sixteen ethnic groups, dominated by the Bushongo. *Bushongo* means "knife throwers." Despite their warrior name, the Kuba are actually renowned throughout Africa for their artwork, especially their raffia cloth.

Above: **This Congolese woman is embroidering Kuba cloth.**

Raffia cloth is generally used to make skirts that are wrapped around the waist, layer upon layer, to create a bulky look. Women's skirts can reach up to 25 feet (7.6 m) in length, and men's skirts can reach up to 30 feet (9 m). The skirts are worn only for special occasions, such as funerals, when they adorn not only the mourners but also the corpse. The Kuba also trade their cloth to neighboring tribes.

Making the cloth is a complex process that involves both men and women. Men strip the raffia fibers from the raffia palm plants, either by hand or with a comb. They then use a loom to weave the fibers into cloth panels.

Women decorate the cloth with embroidery, appliqué, patchwork, and earth-colored dyes. Sometimes a woman works on a series of cloth panels separately and sews them together later to make the skirt. More frequently, one woman is in charge of a group working together on a single skirt. While each woman works on her own panel, the woman in charge makes all of the artistic decisions. She determines, for example, which of the embroidery patterns to use. Each embroidery pattern is composed of various motifs, such as leaflike shapes called *kash* (CASH). One motif is called "tail of the dog" because of the way it curves. Sometimes the entire skirt is covered with embroidery, and other times only part of it is.

The borders of the skirt can be embroidered with dyed raffia thread, sewn in a way that looks like velvet. This type of Kuba cloth is called Kasai velvet and is named after the region in which the Kuba live.

Women tend to engage in this time-consuming process during mourning periods. These periods can last from three to nine months.

Opposite: **This beautiful sample of Kuba cloth, made from raffia fibers, sports a geometric design.**

Léopold II and Sir Henry Morton Stanley

Born in Wales in 1841, famed explorer Henry Morton Stanley began life as John Rowlands. Rowlands worked as a cabin boy on a ship bound for New Orleans, where he met a kindly merchant who adopted him, giving Rowlands his name. Stanley served as a soldier in the Confederate Army during the American Civil War. Later, he became a reporter for *The New York Herald.* The newspaper sent Stanley to Africa to locate David Livingstone, an explorer who had disappeared in 1871 while trying to find the source of the Nile. Stanley found the lost explorer, and, with the famous question, "Dr. Livingstone, I presume?" assured his own place in the history books. After Livingstone's death in 1873, Stanley decided to continue exploring Central Africa.

Stanley left Zanzibar, an island off the coast of Tanzania, in East Africa, on November 12, 1874. On a steamboat called the *Lady Alice*, Stanley took three companions on a large and well-stocked expedition. He sailed first down the Lualaba River and then the Congo River, encountering hostile tribes, illness, and accidents along the way. When he finally reached the impassable

Below: **Henry Morton Stanley (*fourth from left*) found Dr. David Livingstone (*fifth from left*) near Ujiji on Lake Tanganyika on November 10, 1871. After nursing Livingstone back to health, Stanley accompanied him on an expedition to explore Lake Tanganyika.**

Livingstone (now Inga) Falls, he walked the remaining 300 miles (483 km) to the Atlantic Ocean. Stanley was exhausted and sick. His companions and most of the expedition had died. The surviving handful reached the coast on August 12, 1877, two years and nine months after starting.

Stanley was an international hero. To his shock and dismay, however, only King Léopold II of Belgium was interested in his findings. During the preceding centuries, the major European powers had grabbed most of the land in Asia and South America. Only the fate of Central Africa remained undecided, and Léopold did everything in his power to claim the Congo region. He formed the International African Association in 1876 to explore the area. He hired Stanley to develop the region in his name, building a railroad around Livingstone Falls and establishing a series of trading posts along the Congo River as far as Kisangani. Léopold even lobbied the British and U.S. governments to recognize his claim.

At last, Léopold succeeded. He was granted the Congo Free State at the Berlin West Africa Conference, held between 1884 and 1885, in which Central and West Africa were carved into colonies. As for Stanley, he left the Congo in 1884. He later returned to Britain and won a seat in the British Parliament in 1895. Stanley was knighted by the British monarch, Queen Victoria, in 1899. Sir Henry Morton Stanley died in 1904.

Above: **Henry Morton Stanley (***left***) and the ambitious Léopold II, King of Belgium, (***right***) were instrumental in the events leading to the Scramble for Africa, the race by European powers to lay claim to African territories in the late nineteenth and early twentieth centuries.**

THE "BREAKER OF ROCKS"

Stanley's work to open the Lower Congo to commerce earned him the African nickname *Bula Matari* (BULL-ah MAH-tah-REE), or "Breaker of Rocks." This nickname aptly reflected his ruthlessness in crushing all opposition from local African tribes.

60

Masks

Masks are one of the most dramatic art forms in Congo-Kinshasa. They are used throughout the country in an endless variety of traditional rituals and ceremonies, ranging from boyhood initiations to rain dances.

While some masks cover the entire face or just the eyes, others rest on the head like a helmet. The masks can be realistic representations of human faces or bodies or exaggerated representations in which, for instance, the nose is too big or the eyes too small. Alternatively, they may also be symbolic representations of human faces in which, for example, a line symbolizes the eye or the nose. Other masks represent animals or have combinations of human and animal features. The masks are usually made out of wood and are often adorned with beads, hair, skins of animals, or cloth. Certain masks can be worn only by royalty or religious officials; others only by men or only by women.

The Kuba are considered to be some of the best carvers in Africa. They use a series of three masks in public ceremonies, initiations, and funerals. Each mask represents characters in mythical history. Two of them, *mashamboy* (MAH-shahm-boy) and *ngady a mwaash* (in-GAH-dee ahm-wahsh), represent Woot, the founder of the Kuba, and Mweel, his sister or wife. Sometimes the Kuba king wears these masks in ceremonies to symbolize his link to the past and to emphasize the basis of his authority. The third mask is called *bwoom* (buh-WOOM), and it represents a rival of Woot.

The best-known Songe mask is the *kifwebe* (keef-WEB-ay) mask, which is used in ceremonies to celebrate the arrival of dignitaries. The kifwebe is also worn at the funerals of important people in the village. The mask is spherical, like a helmet, except that the back of the head is exposed, while the face is not. Painted red, black, and white stripes curve around the mask according to the contours of carved grooves.

The Western world has long appreciated Congolese masks for their beauty, but, to the Congolese, it makes no sense to consider a mask just a work of art. To them, it is part of a costume that is worn when participating in a particular ceremony. The ritual's mask, costume, dance, and music all go together.

Above: **This Pende mask fits over the head like a helmet. Boys wear these masks during their initiation ceremonies. The masks have facial forms that repeat the angular pattern established by the heavy triangular eyelids. They are covered with raffia. Pende masks are among the most dramatic works of African art.**

Opposite: **The kifwebe mask combines human and animal features. The exaggerated forms of human and animal figures distinguish Congolese art from West African art.**

Mining

Copper: Basis of the Congolese Economy

Congo-Kinshasa's economy has long been dependent on copper, its principal product. The copper reserves in the Katanga region, the center of the copper industry, are estimated to be among the largest in the world. The Katanga region was formerly called Shaba, meaning "copper" in Swahili.

In 1966, Mobutu took over the mining concessions of the privately owned Belgian-based Union Minière du Haut Katanga. These concessions were turned over to a state-owned corporation called Générale des Carrières et des Mines (Gécamines), and the country grew wealthy on copper for almost a decade.

When copper prices collapsed in 1974, the Congolese economy collapsed with them. The immediate impact was devastating. Foreign investment eventually revived the industry, and the region once again produced 60 percent of the world's copper. Until the late 1980s, mining accounted for at least three-fourths of the country's earnings from exports.

Left: Copper mining in the Katanga region has long been Congo-Kinshasa's main source of income. Apart from copper, Katanga also boasts extensive zinc, silver, gold, coal, manganese, and platinum deposits.

In the early 1990s, a combination of corruption, mismanagement, and withdrawal of foreign aid resulted in the complete disintegration of the copper mining industry. Output fell dramatically. The already weak Congolese economy crashed. The 1994 to 1997 rebellion only made the situation worse. Equipment was smashed, and mines were flooded. After 1997, copper accounted for 38 percent of the income Congo-Kinshasa earned through exports, and foreign companies were trying to revive Gécamines. Today, these efforts are on hold, as rebel factions occupy the primary copper-producing regions and mine the Congolese riches for themselves.

A Haven for Minerals

The mineral deposits of Congo-Kinshasa include more than just copper. The Katanga region has vast reserves of cobalt. Geologists estimate that the region contains about 65 percent of the world's total. In the late 1980s, more than 50 percent of the world's cobalt was mined in Katanga.

The Kasai-Oriental region is a leading center for industrial diamonds. Before the civil wars, the region produced one-third of the world's supply of industrial diamonds. These diamonds are mined both by companies and by villagers, who sneak into unguarded valleys and scrape away at the red dusty dirt.

Other regions in Congo-Kinshasa are also rich in minerals. Nord- and Sud-Kivu have large reserves of cassiterite and gold.

Mobutu Sese Seko

It is impossible to think of Congo-Kinshasa without thinking of Mobutu Sese Seko, the dictator who ruled the country from 1965 to 1997.

Mobutu took power in 1965, after overthrowing President Kasavubu in a coup. In 1970, he was officially elected president. As head of a one-party state, he suppressed tribal conflicts and encouraged a sense of nationhood. At the same time, he amassed a vast personal fortune, believed to have peaked at U.S. $4 billion in the 1980s, and corruption became widespread.

Although the constitution required that presidential elections be held every seven years, Mobutu never faced any opposition. This was not because he was a popular ruler. He faced no opposition because he used his intelligence services to crush political dissent and silence his critics. Even when the continued economic deterioration and unrest of 1991 led him to agree to share power with political opponents, Mobutu still attempted to oppose change.

Left: Mobutu addresses attendees at a rally held during the annual independence celebrations. After seizing power, he established a presidential form of government headed by himself. He then began dismantling the republic. He changed the country in all but name from a republic to an estate, just as it had been under King Léopold II. The hallmarks of Mobutu's regime were political repression and corruption.

Left: **During Mobutu's rule, it was very common for the Congolese to wear clothes depicting the face of their leader. Despite this apparent display of patriotism, the Congolese people feared Mobutu, even though they often called him "Uncle Mo."**

Kleptocracy

Another hallmark of Mobutu's regime was corruption. The greed and bribery started at the top and filtered down through every level of the government. Ministers demanded money for government contracts. Civil servants expected a bribe before processing paperwork. Even the police were corrupt. Often they set up roadblocks and demanded a payoff before letting motorists through. Describing the situation in Zaire, the international press coined the word "kleptocracy," from the word *kleptomania*, meaning an irresistible impulse to steal.

Mobutu skimmed profits from mining exports, among other things, and spent the money lavishly on himself and his friends. He built extravagant palaces all over the country and bought several châteaus in Europe, including one in Switzerland.

Mobutu rebuilt his birthplace, Gbadolite, in northern Zaire. He made the town of 20,000 the proud owners of the only four-lane highway in the entire country. With an international airport, luxury residences, and a huge modern hospital, Gbadolite stood in stark contrast to neighboring villages of mud huts and malnourished children.

Patrice Lumumba and Congolese Nationalism

Born in 1925, Patrice Lumumba attended a Protestant mission school. He then entered the colonial civil service. His career in politics began a few years later.

Inspired by the events in neighboring countries in the 1950s, the Congolese began to campaign for their own independence. Lumumba proved to be a vital part of that campaign. In 1958, he founded the Congolese National Movement (MNC), the first nationwide Congolese political party.

In 1959, the Belgian government announced a program for independence, and in January 1960, it hosted a Round Table Conference in Brussels, Belgium. Representatives of all the Congolese parties discussed what kind of government an independent Congo should have. Many of these men, including Joseph Kasavubu, wanted a federal system, distributing power among a central government and the territories under it. Lumumba, on the other hand, wanted a united Congo under a strong central government. The Belgians favored Lumumba's plan.

National elections were held in May 1960. Although Lumumba's MNC did better than any other party, it failed to

PAN-AFRICANISM

Patrice Lumumba, who came from the small and politically insignificant Batetela tribe, was a fervent advocate of Pan-Africanism. He believed that all African nations should form alliances with one another.

Left: On July 1, 1960, Belgian prime minister Gaston Eyskens (*center*) signed the papers that gave the Republic of the Belgian Congo its independence. Patrice Lumumba, the new Congolese prime minister, is seated on the extreme left.

Left: **Outrage at Lumumba's death went beyond territorial boundaries. Many of his supporters vented their frustration toward U.N. Secretary-General Dag Hammarskjöld and Congolese president Kasavubu. Today, Lumumba is seen as a national hero, even by his old enemies, and he continues to inspire African nationalists.**

win a majority. The MNC was forced to form a coalition, or union, with another political party, Alliance of the Bakongo (ABAKO). Lumumba became prime minister, and his opponent, Kasavubu, became president. The country, however, fell apart quickly. A few days after independence, the army revolted. Then the mineral-rich province of Katanga seceded from the country. Belgium sent in troops, claiming that the Belgians in the region needed protection, but in reality, they were supporting the rebellion.

Lumumba first appealed to the United Nations (U.N.) to help reestablish order. While the U.N. did send troops, they refused to quell the rebellion. Next, Lumumba asked the Soviet Union for help. This move deeply alarmed the West, especially the United States, and the crisis in the new Republic of the Congo began to unfold on the world stage. The Cold War was at its height, and the United States was worried about Soviet influence in the newly emerging countries of Africa. Supported by the United States, Kasavubu took action. He dismissed Lumumba who, in turn, dismissed him. For a brief period, the country had two governments. On September 14, 1960, Colonel Joseph Mobutu seized power and set up a new government with Kasavubu. Lumumba was captured and taken to the province of Katanga. He was assassinated on January 17, 1961.

Rebellion and Civil War

General Laurent Kabila led the Alliance of Democratic Forces for the Liberation of the Congo (AFDL). Backed by neighboring Rwanda, Uganda, and Burundi, the AFDL overthrew President Mobutu in May 1997. Kabila, however, soon began to face troubles of his own. His reversal of fortune as the new president of Congo-Kinshasa began in August 1998, when he dismissed the various foreign troops and advisers (mainly Rwandan) who had helped him take power. Their presence in the government had angered many Congolese.

Tutsi-led Rwanda and Burundi, still anxious to curb Hutu activity in Congo-Kinshasa, then joined forces with three Congolese rebel groups already fighting to overthrow Kabila. Uganda followed in support of Rwanda. Meanwhile, Kabila allied himself with his former enemies, the Hutu militiamen responsible for the 1994 Rwandan genocide and indigenous warriors, called the *mayi-mayi* (MAH-hee MAH-hee). He also is now supported by Angola, Chad, Namibia, Sudan, and Zimbabwe. Together, pro-

Below: After the 1994 Rwandan genocide, many refugees fled to Nord- and Sud-Kivu. In an attempt to alleviate the strain on the local economies there, the Zairian government expelled over 75,000 Rwandan Hutus within one month.

Left: Although the Congolese population greeted Laurent Kabila's seizure of power with much optimism, he has since shown himself to be as oppressive as his predecessor. He has arbitrarily arrested, tortured, and killed thousands of civilians.

Kabila forces started an ethnic war in eastern Congo-Kinshasa against Congolese Tutsi, but they quickly lost. Anti-Kabila forces not only pushed them out of the area, but these forces also went on to conquer the eastern and northeastern parts of the country.

Africa's First World War

The current situation in Congo-Kinshasa is enormously complex. The war has spread beyond the Congo and the Great Lakes Region and is now being called "Africa's first world war." At least six foreign states are actively involved in the civil war, with a total of 35,000 troops fighting. Nine rebel groups based in Congo-Kinshasa aim to overthrow neighboring states. For all, the great prize is Congo-Kinshasa's fantastic mineral wealth, which foreign armies have been looting.

The true losers of the conflict are the Congolese people. An estimated 1.75 million fighters, civilians, and refugees have been killed since the fighting began. Hundreds of thousands more have been uprooted. Elephants and gorillas are being poached or hunted for food. The country's economy, which was in trouble when Kabila took office, is now in ruins.

U.N. INTERVENTION

On June 16, 2000, the U.N. Security Council passed a resolution demanding an end to the fighting and the immediate withdrawal of Rwandan and Ugandan troops, as well as all other forces, from Congo-Kinshasa. The U.N., however, stopped short of setting a deadline and only hinted at imposing sanctions if the parties did not comply. The resolution was sparked by a general disregard of the Lusaka Peace Agreement, signed in July 1999, and by heavy fighting between Rwandan and Ugandan forces in Kisangani, which left over 150 civilians dead. U.N. military observers reported on June 17, 2000, that the Rwandan army had withdrawn from Kisangani, and that Ugandan forces were pulling out. The U.N., however, will only deploy a peacekeeping force into Congo-Kinshasa when the safety of its troops can be guaranteed.

Riverboats

At the time of its independence from Belgium, Congo-Kinshasa had a passable road system. It was conceivable, at least, to drive from one side of the country to the other. Now such a journey would be impossible. Today, only 1,914 miles (3,080 km) of 95,708 miles (153,994 km) of road are paved throughout the entire nation. Many of these are impassable during the rainy season. The railways have not fared much better. Now less than 10 percent of Congo-Kinshasa's original 3,193 miles (5,138 km) of tracks remains usable. What is left are the waterways. Most Congolese travel from one major city to another on one of the riverboats that sail along the Congo River. These riverboats have often been called "traveling markets" or "floating cities."

A riverboat consists of a large, four-decked steamboat that carries passengers traveling first class. Most passengers, however, have to settle for cheaper and more primitive accommodations in one of the barges that the steamer pulls behind it.

On these barges, passengers live out their lives as if they were at home. Music, both live and from passengers' radios, blasts twenty-four hours a day. Women, who have hauled on board not only food for the journey but also mortars and pestles, spend a lot of their time pounding cassava. They cook over open fires. Quarters soon develop, with each family or group occupying the same place for the duration of the journey, which can be quite long. The trip from Kinshasa to Kisangani takes almost two weeks.

The decks are also packed with animals, both dead and alive, from chickens, pigs, and monkeys to porcupines, aardvarks, and crocodiles. Some animals come aboard as food for the journey. Others are to be sold.

Commerce is a constant feature of these river trips. Merchants set up permanent stalls on the decks, where they sell anything from razor blades to monkey stew. They are joined by hundreds of villagers who row up to the steamer in their pirogues, or dugout canoes, to sell their wares, such as cassava, woven mats, and parrots, to passengers. There may be over one hundred canoes tied to the steamer at any one time. When the villagers finish selling their goods, they simply paddle home.

Above: **A traveling saleswoman tries to sell a freshly caught fish to a passenger on a riverboat.**

Opposite: **During the long journey on the Congo River, pirogues attach themselves to the riverboat, while their owners try to tempt passengers into buying their wares.**

71

Soukous

Soukous developed in the 1950s, when Latin American and Caribbean rumbas were all the rage among the Belgians living in Kinshasa and other Congolese cities. Several local bands began to Africanize the rumba by adding African melodies and rhythms. The result was the African rumba or Soukous, which comes from the French word *secouer* (SEH-coo-eh), meaning "to shake." The lyrics to Soukous are generally written in French or Lingala, although some are in Tshiluba. Soukous became a popular dance style in the 1960s, but its name soon came to represent all African rumbas.

The Sorcerer of the Guitar

One of the most important Soukous musicians of all time is Franco Luambo (1938–1989). His charm and guitar skills earned him the title "the sorcerer of the guitar," as well as accolades, such as *le Grand Maître* (LUH grahn MAY-truh), or the Great Master. Although his father wanted him to become a doctor, Luambo spent much of his childhood in the marketplace, playing a guitar he had made out of tin cans. At the age of twelve, he debuted with Watem, one of the most important bands of the time. In 1956, he founded

Left: **The Congolese loved Franco Luambo's songs for their social commentary, their well-adapted band arrangements, and the emotional sound of his guitar and voice.**

LE GRAND MAITRE FRANCO
INTERPELLE LA SOCIETE
DANS
"ATTENTION NA SIDA"

Left: **Luambo's music conveyed important social messages. This record is called, "Watch out for AIDS."**

his own band, called Le tout puissant O.K. Jazz (The All Powerful O.K. Jazz). The band went on to make over one hundred records and dominate the Soukous scene for more than thirty-five years.

Luambo used his music to comment on social problems, such as the spread of AIDS and relationships between the sexes. In his album *12,600 lettres à Franco* (*12,600 Letters to Franco*), Luambo reads imaginary letters from women seeking advice. Many concern the emotional pain women feel when their husbands take additional wives. His portrayal of women, however, prompted some Congolese feminists to label him sexist. For example, M'Blia Bel, one of the country's best known female singers, often took issue with Franco's opinions in her own work.

By the 1970s, Luambo and his contemporaries, including Tabu Ley Rochereau, regularly topped the pop charts in both Central and West Africa, where Soukous greatly influenced the development of popular music. Today, Soukous is increasingly popular in the West, especially in France, where many of the more successful Soukous musicians have made their home.

In 1978, Mobutu decorated Luambo for his contribution to the development of Zaire's musical heritage. Although Luambo openly supported Mobutu and campaigned for him during elections, Congolese of diverse political views revered the sorcerer of the guitar. Luambo died on October 12, 1989.

RELATIONS WITH NORTH AMERICA

Until recently, North America was extremely important to the political destiny of Congo-Kinshasa. The United States was Mobutu's greatest ally during his thirty-two-year regime, and it supported him against a number of insurrections and invasions. Since the end of the Cold War, however, North American relations with Congo-Kinshasa have not been so warm.

Nevertheless, solid humanitarian links remain. Both the U.S. and Canadian governments are involved in sending humanitarian aid to those most affected by the current civil war. Furthermore, North American aid agencies have a long history of working in Congo-Kinshasa and have improved the Congolese people's quality of life.

Despite such political and humanitarian ties, however, North American culture has not had as big an impact on Congolese culture as it has had on others. In fact, if anything, the situation is just the reverse. For a country as underdeveloped and as isolated as Congo-Kinshasa, its culture has had a lasting impact on North American culture, especially in terms of the arts.

Opposite: **A male pygmy in the Ituri Forest watches a tourist use a bow and arrow.**

Left: **North Americans and Europeans who come to Congo-Kinshasa as professionals or volunteers with development agencies have played a significant role in educating the Congolese population.**

Left: John F. Kennedy (*left*), 35th president of the United States, and Zairian soldier and politician Joseph Mobutu (*right*), commander-in-chief of the Congolese armed forces, meet at the White House in Washington, D.C., on June 4, 1963.

Mobutu and the Cold War

Relations between the United States and the Democratic Republic of the Congo became close after Mobutu Sese Seko came to power in 1965. Throughout his rule, Mobutu was fully aware of the importance of U.S. backing.

During the late 1960s, Mobutu's regime received U.S. support in various economic and political disputes. In the early 1970s, however, Zaire distanced itself from the United States and joined other sub-Saharan states in breaking relations with Israel over its occupation of Egyptian territory. In 1975, the United States and Zaire supported the same faction in the Angolan civil war. It was then that the United States recognized Zaire as an important stabilizing factor in Central Africa.

U.S. relations changed with the Carter administration. Its first priority in foreign policy was the promotion of human rights. This policy proved a problem for the Mobutu regime because of its poor human rights record. This attitude changed with the second invasion of Katanga in 1978. President Jimmy Carter supported Mobutu's accusations that Cuba and the Soviet Union were involved. The United States, however, did not become involved militarily, sending only medical and transportation supplies.

Mobutu welcomed the election of Ronald Reagan and then George Bush to the U.S. presidency. Once again, he was seen as supporting the United States in its fight against the Soviet Union.

RED RUBBER

During the era of the Congo Free State, when Léopold II ruled the country as if it were his personal plantation, the documentation of Belgian atrocities by two African-Americans was very important. Due in part to the work of George Washington Williams, a journalist, and Reverend William Sheppard, a missionary, the English writer E. D. Morel (1873–1924) was able to write *Red Rubber* and shake the conscience of the world against the king of Belgium.

The End of an Era

It was only after the end of the Cold War, with the breakup of the Soviet bloc in 1989, that the United States stepped up its criticism of Mobutu's regime. In 1990, the American Congress cut military and economic aid to Zaire because of Mobutu's human rights record and the likelihood that his vast wealth had been stolen from the Zairian people.

The United States, together with other countries, attempted to promote peaceful political change in Zaire through a democratic transition to fair and free multiparty elections and a democratically elected government. Frustrated by Mobutu's obstruction of this transition process, the United States downgraded its diplomatic presence in Kinshasa; the U.S. embassy was headed by a chargé d'affaires instead of an ambassador between March 1993 and November 1995. In June 1993, President Bill Clinton announced the suspension of entry into the United States of people who developed or implemented policies that stopped Zaire's transition to democracy. Following the formation of a transitional parliament (the HCR-PT) in 1994 and the establishment of the National Electoral Commission (CNE) in 1995, the United States appointed an ambassador to Zaire in November 1995. The United States, however, made it clear that closer U.S.-Zairian relations depended upon the successful transition to a democratic government and free elections by July 1997.

Left: **President Mobutu (***left***) meets U.S. president George Bush (***right***) in the Oval Office at the White House in Washington, D.C., on June 29, 1989.**

Current Relations

In January 2000, Richard C. Holbrooke, the American representative to the United Nations, persuaded all the leaders of the countries involved in Congo-Kinshasa's fighting to attend a special Security Council session in New York. During the session, the African leaders recommitted themselves to the Lusaka Peace Agreement, signed in July 1999. As a general disregard for this agreement continued, the U.N. Security Council issued a resolution in June 2000, demanding a withdrawal of all external forces from Congo-Kinshasa. This move was supported by the U.S. and Canadian governments. Furthermore, President Clinton supported a proposal to send U.N. peace monitors and peacekeeping troops into the region as soon as their safety could be guaranteed.

The United States still maintains trading ties with Congo-Kinshasa. The United States is Congo-Kinshasa's second-largest trading partner, absorbing 22 percent of the country's exports. The United States imports more than it exports to Congo-Kinshasa. These imports are mainly coffee and minerals, such as copper, cobalt, and diamonds. The United States exports primarily food and machinery to Congo-Kinshasa.

Left: U.N. Secretary-General Kofi Annan (*left*) greets U.S. Secretary of State Madeleine Albright (*right*) before their meeting at the United Nations in New York on January 24, 2000. Albright chaired the U.N. Security Council session on the civil war in Congo-Kinshasa.

Left: **A doctor who works for the World Health Organization (WHO) examines a malnourished Congolese man.**

Development Agencies

Most North Americans living in Congo-Kinshasa are attached to development agencies. These agencies, such as Save the Children and the United Nations Children's Fund (UNICEF), work to raise literacy levels, improve health care systems, and increase the nation's food supply. Hundreds of Americans work in Congo-Kinshasa on projects sponsored by the United States Agency for International Development (USAID).

The U.S. and Canadian governments are currently contributing to international efforts to send food and supplies to help regions most devastated by the civil war. With war engulfing much of the country, reconstruction and development have been heavily disrupted. Nevertheless, development agencies are looking into ways of continuing their work on immunizing children, combating the spread of the HIV virus, and strengthening the health care infrastructure. It remains to be seen, however, whether their efforts will have an impact on a country and people torn apart by civil war.

NATIONAL IMMUNIZATION DAYS (NIDS) IN CONGO-KINSHASA

USAID and the World Health Organization (WHO), together with the Congolese Ministry of Health, organized National Immunization Days in 1999 to vaccinate children under the age of five against polio. The program was only partially successful, as 36.2 percent of children under the age of five were not immunized due to security problems. The organizers remain unfazed and hope to conduct the campaign again in the near future.

Immigration to North America

Between 1987 and 1997, 2,743 Congolese immigrated to the United States. The majority of these immigrants went to live in big cities. In 1997, the largest portion of Congolese settled in the Washington, D.C., area, where a number of vibrant African communities exist. Other large Congolese communities are in New York, Boston, and Los Angeles. Congolese immigrants have settled not only along the East Coast but all over the United States. Small Congolese communities can be found in cities as far apart as Detroit, Michigan, and Dallas, Texas.

While only 770 Congolese immigrated to Canada between 1981 and 1990, almost three and half times that number came over the next five years. Between 1991 and 1996, Canada welcomed 2,695 new Congolese immigrants, bringing the total Canadian Congolese population to 5,390. Sixty percent of these people live in Québec, primarily in Montréal, where French is spoken. The second- and third-largest communities are in Toronto and Ottawa, respectively.

REMEMBER LUMUMBA DAY

Every January, the "Remember Lumumba" event is held in San Francisco, California, to commemorate the life of Patrice Lumumba, the first prime minister of the Republic of the Congo. The organizers of the event are the International Patrice Lumumba Society, the Committee for South African Solidarity, and African Sun Publishing. The event also commemorates the birth of U.S. civil rights leader Dr. Martin Luther King, Jr.

Immigration and Basketball

One of Congo-Kinshasa's finest exports to the United States in recent years has been its basketball players. One of these players is 7-foot, 2-inch (2.18-m) Dikembe Mutombo, a center for the National Basketball Association's Atlanta Hawks. Mutombo came to the United States in 1987 to play for Georgetown University. He is from Kinshasa, where most of his family still lives.

Despite his success in the United States, Mutombo has not forgotten his homeland. He started a bus company in Kinshasa to ease the transportation burden caused by the city's ever-growing population. In August 1999, he returned to Congo-Kinshasa as part of an effort to raise U.S. $50 million to build a 250-bed hospital in Kinshasa.

Mutombo is also a big supporter of Congolese basketball. He paid for the uniforms, equipment, and even the airfare of the national women's team, so that they could attend the 1996 Summer Olympic Games in Atlanta, Georgia.

Several of those Olympians came to the United States to stay. They include Tshijuka "Mamissa" Mwenentanda, the 6-foot, 5-inch (1.95-m) forward from Lubumbashi.

Left: Dikembe Mutombo, the center for the Atlanta Hawks, claps during the welcoming ceremony for Zaire's Olympic team at the Olympic Village in Atlanta, Georgia, on July 17, 1996.

Opposite: A pro-government supporter, originally from Congo-Kinshasa, waves his homeland's flag in front of a police officer during a protest in Moncton, New Brunswick, at the VIIIe Sommet de la Francophonie (Eighth World Francophone Summit) on September 4, 1999.

Academic Ties

Founded in 1961, the American School of Kinshasa (TASOK) is a private school that caters to overseas students at elementary, middle, and high school levels. Alumni from the school work in all regions of the globe, and all carry the experience of living in the heart of Africa.

The American University of Kinshasa was founded in 1994 by graduates of U.S. universities. The university was established for African students, international students, and American exchange programs, as well as for organizations and corporations interested in Congo-Kinshasa and Africa as a whole. One of the American University's aims is to promote awareness of cultural, educational, and trade exchange opportunities between Africa and the United States.

North American-Congolese Ties via the Internet

Many North American Congolese keep communication lines open with fellow Congolese still living in Congo-Kinshasa via discussion groups on the Internet. Zaire-List (now called Congo-L) was created in August 1994 as the first discussion group that enables members of the Congolese community in North America to discuss issues related to their homeland with their counterparts in Congo-Kinshasa.

ANACCO

ANACCO, the All North America Conference on the Congo, is a nonprofit organization that enables Congolese within Congo-Kinshasa and Congolese groups living in North America to discuss the political, social, and economic problems of Congo-Kinshasa. ANACCO's main aims are to help reconstruct Congo-Kinshasa and support the country's transition to democracy. The organization was set up following a conference held at the University of Kentucky in April 1996. Today, ANACCO has executive committees in the United States, Canada, and France.

Literature

Prestigious American authors have been influenced by the hardships the Congolese endured during Belgian colonial rule, as well as by their exotic mysteries and rituals. At the turn of the twentieth century, Mark Twain (1835–1910) wrote his famous *King Léopold's Soliloquy* (1905), which denounced the colonial domination of the Congo Free State and its peoples. More recently, San Francisco journalist Adam Hochschild (1942–) wrote *King Léopold's Ghost: A Story of Greed, Terror, and Heroism in Colonial Africa* (1998), a book that recounts the quiet genocide that occurred in the Congo Free State during King Léopold II's rule between 1880 and 1908. The book earned Hochschild the Canadian Lionel Gelber Foundation Prize for best book on international relations in 1999.

Famous author Michael Crichton (1942–), who wrote *Jurassic Park*, wrote *Congo* (1980), a thriller about an expedition that sets out to discover why an earlier expedition was mysteriously wiped out while looking for industrial diamonds in Zaire.

Below: **Popular U.S. authors Mark Twain (*left*) and Michael Crichton (*right*) have used Congo-Kinshasa as the subject for some of their works.**

Afropop in North America

In 1986, singer and songwriter Paul Simon introduced many Americans to African pop music for the first time with his *Graceland* album. The Grammy-winning album and Simon's subsequent tours also introduced African musicians to America. One of these is Congolese Dominic Kanza, who migrated to the United States in 1989.

Kanza was born in Zaire but raised in London, England, for twelve years before returning to his homeland. He is now one of the foremost practitioners of Soukous guitar in America.

Left: Paul Simon's *Graceland* album has sold over 14 million copies and was named Album of the Year at the 1986 Grammy Awards. Simon brought key African musicians to New York and London to complete the recording of the album and later toured with them. The songs on the album merge African rhythms with Simon's personal musical style.

Left: Dominic Kanza (*center*) is the band-leader, singer, and lead guitarist of his band, the African Rhythm Machine. His music draws from the guitar-driven Soukous sound that put his native Congo-Kinshasa on the musical map. It also incorporates West-African drumming and touches of American funk and jazz.

Since coming to the United States, Kanza has collaborated with Paul Simon on numerous projects, including President Clinton's Inaugural Ball and Simon's annual "Back at the Ranch" concert series, sharing the stage with performers such as Billy Joel and James Taylor. He also worked with Simon on his *Rhythm of the Saints* album, playing lead guitar on two tracks. He has collaborated with composer Bob Telson on countless projects, including the Broadway musical *Chronicle of a Death Foretold*.

Kanza has performed with an impressive roster of musicians that includes jazz legends Wynton Marsalis, Pharaoh Sanders, and Michael Brecker and rock stars Bruce Springsteen and Jon Bon Jovi. He has also written and performed one of the theme songs for *The Oprah Winfrey Show*.

Other renowned Congolese Soukous performers in the United States include Diblo Dibala and his acclaimed Soukous band Matchatcha. Dibala first toured in the United States with his previous band, Loketo. These tours introduced Soukous to a new American audience, paving the way for countless other Soukous artists. Dibala and Matchatcha frequently play in large U.S. cities, such as New York, Dallas, and Chicago.

CUBISM

Congo-Kinshasa's arts had a great impact on western artistic tradition. At the beginning of the twentieth century, a new artistic style known as cubism changed art forever. The founders of cubism were heavily influenced by the Congolese use of symbolism and the shapes and appearance of Congolese masks. Russian-born U.S. painter and sculptor Max Weber (1881–1961) helped to introduce cubism to the United States. His cubist works include *Chinese Restaurant* (1915).

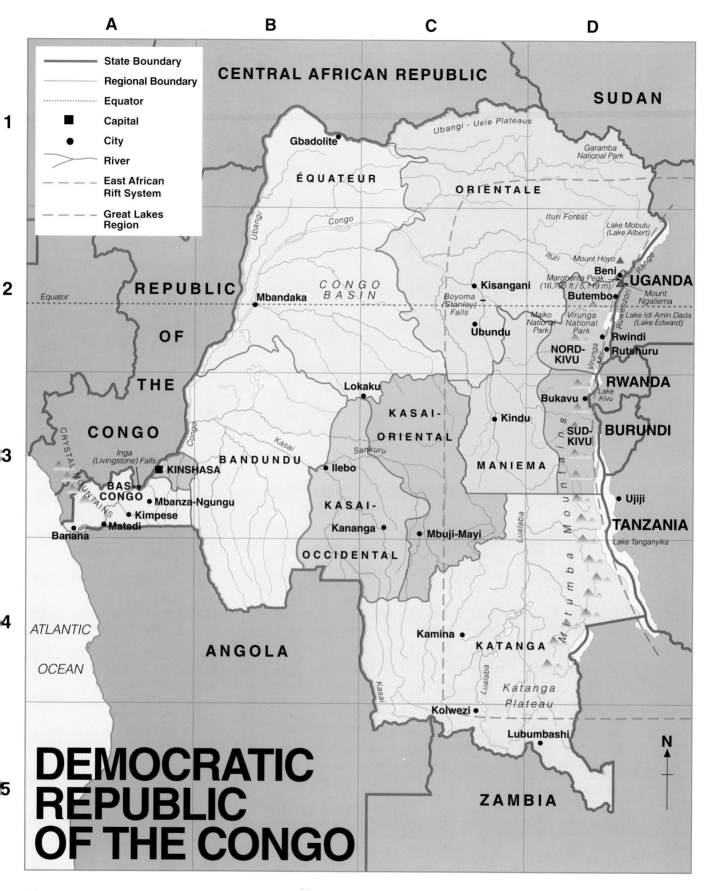

DEMOCRATIC REPUBLIC OF THE CONGO

A **B** **C** **D**

1
2
3
4
5

State Boundary
Regional Boundary
Equator
■ Capital
● City
River
East African Rift System
Great Lakes Region

CENTRAL AFRICAN REPUBLIC

SUDAN

Ubangi - Uele Plateaus

Garamba National Park

Gbadolite

ÉQUATEUR

ORIENTALE

Ituri Forest

Lake Mobutu (Lake Albert)

Congo

Ubangi

REPUBLIC

Equator

OF

THE

Mbandaka

CONGO BASIN

Ituri

Mount Hoyo

Margherita Peak (16,795 ft / 5,119 m)

Beni

Butembo

UGANDA

Mount Ngaliema

Boyoma (Stanley) Falls

Kisangani

Lake Idi Amin Dada (Lake Edward)

Ubundu

Maiko National Park

Virunga National Park

Rwindi

Rutshuru

NORD-KIVU

Virunga Mts.

Ruwenzori Range

CONGO

Lokaku

KASAI-ORIENTAL

Kindu

Bukavu

Lake Kivu

RWANDA

CRYSTAL MOUNTAINS

Inga (Livingstone) Falls

Congo

Kasai

Sankuru

SUD-KIVU

BURUNDI

KINSHASA

BANDUNDU

Ilebo

MANIEMA

Ujiji

BAS-CONGO

Mbanza-Ngungu

Kimpese

KASAI-

Kananga

Mbuji-Mayi

Mitumba Mountains

TANZANIA

Matadi

Lualaba

Lake Tanganyika

Banana

OCCIDENTAL

ATLANTIC

OCEAN

ANGOLA

Kasai

Kamina

KATANGA

Lualaba

Katanga Plateau

Kolwezi

Lubumbashi

N

ZAMBIA

86

Above: Rutshuru in the Virunga Mountains is home to some beautiful waterfalls.

Angola A3-C5
Atlantic Ocean A3-A5

Banana A3
Bandundu Region B2-B4
Bas-Congo Region A3
Beni D2
Boyoma (Stanley)
    Falls C2
Bukavu D3
Burundi D3
Butembo D2

Central African Republic
    A1-D1
Congo Basin B2-C2
Congo River A3-C2
Crystal Mountains A3

East African Rift System
    D1-D4
Équateur Region B1-C3

Garamba National
    Park D1
Gbadolite B1
Great Lakes Region
    C1-D5

Ilebo B3
Inga (Livingstone)
    Falls A3

Ituri Forest D2
Ituri River D2

Kamina C4
Kananga C3
Kasai River B3-C5
Kasai-Occidental Region
    B3-C4
Kasai-Oriental Region
    C3-C4
Katanga Plateau C4-D5
Katanga Region C4-D5
Kimpese A3
Kindu C3
Kinshasa A3
Kisangani C2
Kolwezi C5

Lake Idi Amin Dada
    (Edward) D2
Lake Kivu D3
Lake Mobutu (Albert) D2
Lake Tanganyika D3-D4
Lokaku C3
Lualaba River C2-C5
Lubumbashi D5

Maiko National Park D2
Maniema Region C2-D3
Margherita Peak D2
Matadi A3
Mbandaka B2

Mbanza-Ngungu A3
Mbuji-Mayi C3
Mitumba Mountains
    D3-D4
Mount Hoyo D2
Mount Ngaliema D2

Nord-Kivu Region D2

Orientale Region C1-D2

Republic of the Congo
    A3-B1
Rutshuru D2
Ruwenzori Range D2
Rwanda D2-D3
Rwindi D2

Sankuru River B3-C4
Sud-Kivu Region D3
Sudan D1

Tanzania D3-D4

Ubangi River B2-C1
Ubangi-Uele Plateaus C1
Ubundu C2
Uganda D1-D2
Ujiji D3

Virunga Mountains D2
Virunga National Park
    D2

Zambia C5-D5

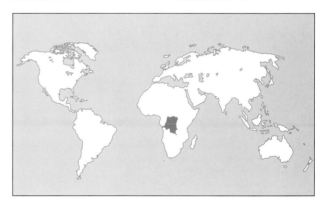

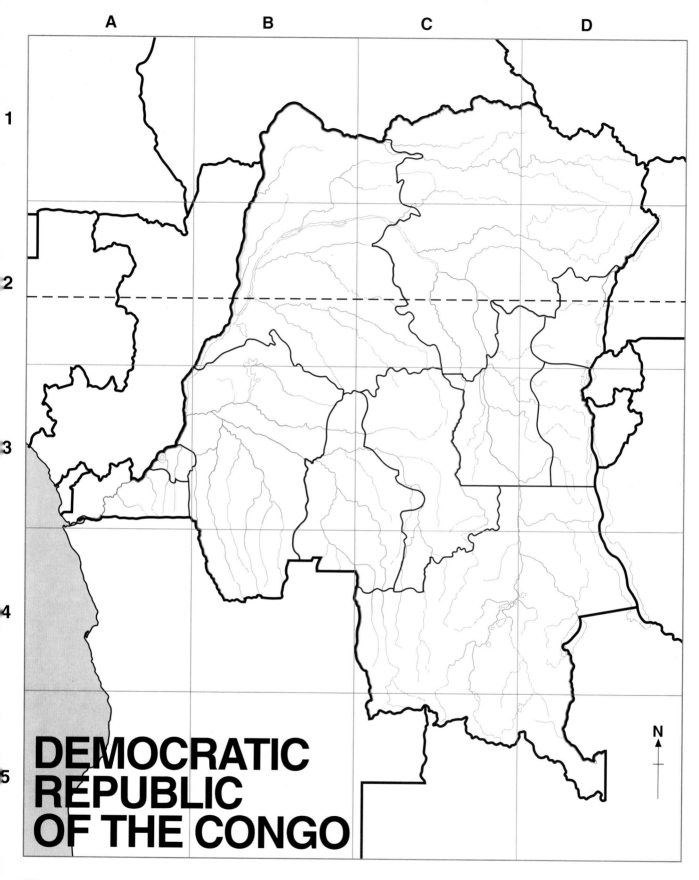

A **B** **C** **D**

1

2

3

4

5

N

DEMOCRATIC REPUBLIC OF THE CONGO

How Is Your Geography?

Learning to identify the main geographical areas and points of a country can be challenging. Although it may seem difficult at first to memorize the locations and spellings of major cities or the names of mountain ranges, rivers, deserts, lakes, and other prominent physical features, the end result of this effort can be very rewarding. Places you previously did not know existed will suddenly come to life when referred to in world news, whether in newspapers, television reports, or other books and reference sources. This knowledge will make you feel a bit closer to the rest of the world, with its fascinating variety of cultures and physical geography.

Used in a classroom setting, the instructor can make duplicates of this map using a copy machine. (PLEASE DO NOT WRITE IN THIS BOOK!) Students can then fill in any requested information on their individual map copies. Used one-on-one, the student can also make copies of the map on a copy machine and use them as a study tool. The student can practice identifying place names and geographical features on his or her own.

Below: **Snakes, such as the green bush viper, are found throughout Congo-Kinshasa.**

The Democratic Republic of the Congo at a Glance

Official Name   Democratic Republic of the Congo (since 1997)

Former Names   Republic of Zaire (1971–1997); Democratic Republic of the Congo (1964–1971); Republic of the Congo (1960–1964); Republic of the Belgian Congo (1908–1960); Congo Free State (1885–1908)

Capital   Kinshasa

Official Language   French

National Languages   Kikongo, Lingala, Swahili, Tshiluba

Population   50,481,305 (1999 estimate)

Land Area   905,564 square miles (2,345,410 square km)

Regions   Bandundu, Bas-Congo, Équateur, Kasai-Occidental, Kasai-Oriental, Katanga, Maniema, Nord-Kivu, Orientale, Sud-Kivu

Highest Point   Margherita Peak   16,795 feet (5,119 m)

Border Countries   Angola, Burundi, Central African Republic, Republic of the Congo, Rwanda, Sudan, Tanzania, Uganda, Zambia

Major Rivers   Congo, Kasai, Lualaba, Ubangi

Major Lakes   Idi Amin Dada (Edward), Kivu, Mobutu (Albert), Tanganyika

Major Cities   Kananga, Kindu, Kinshasa, Kisangani, Kolwezi, Lokaku, Lubumbashi, Mbandaka, Mbuji-Mayi

Major Religions   Islam, Kimbanguism, Protestantism, Roman Catholicism, traditional religions

Main Tribes   Kongo, Luba, Mangbetu-Azande, Mongo

Major Exports   Cobalt, coffee, copper, crude oil, diamonds, gold

Major Imports   Foodstuffs, machinery, transport equipment

Currency   Congolese Franc (CF 685 = U.S. $1 in 2000)

Opposite: **Vendors sell souvenirs along the route to Mount Hoyo in northeastern Congo-Kinshasa.**

Glossary

African Vocabulary

Aka (AH-kah): a pygmy tribe that lives in the Ituri Forest.

Bambuti (BAM-BOOT-ee): the four pygmy tribes that live in the Ituri Forest.

bamiki bandura (bah-MEEK-ee bon-DURE-ah): children of the forest; what the Mbuti pygmies call themselves.

Bila (BEE-lah): an agricultural tribe that trades with the Mbuti.

Bula Matari (BULL-ah MAH-tah-REE): Breaker of Rocks; Sir Henry Morton Stanley's nickname.

Bushongo (BOO-shong-go): knife throwers; refers to the main ethnic group of the Kuba people.

bwoom (buh-WOOM): Kuba mask representing a rival of Woot.

Efe (AY-fay): a pygmy tribe that lives in the Ituri Forest.

kalimba (kah-LIM-bah): lamellaphone or thumb piano made from a piece of wood with metal strips nailed to it.

kash (CASH): Kuba embroidery motif in the form of a leaf.

kifwebe (keef-WEB-ay): Songe mask worn at funerals and in ceremonies celebrating the arrival of dignitaries.

Kinois (KEEN-wah): the inhabitants of Kinshasa.

lusaka (loo-SAH-kah): a memory device used by the Luba oral historian.

mankala (man-KAH-lah): an ancient African game.

mashamboy (MAH-shahm-boy): Kuba mask representing Woot, the founder of the Kuba people.

mayi-mayi (MAH-hee MAH-hee): native warriors who support Laurent Kabila.

Mbuti (em-BOOT-ee): a pygmy tribe that lives in the Ituri Forest.

mdudye (em-DUH-DEE-yay): man of memory; the oral historian of the Luba.

moambé (MOW-am-bay): the Congolese national dish made from chicken cooked in a spicy sauce.

ndura (in-DURE-ah): forestness; the quality worshiped by Mbuti pygmies.

ngady a mwaash (in-GAH-dee ahm-wahsh): Kuba mask representing Mweel, Woot's sister or wife.

Ngunza (in-GUN-zah): prophet or doer of miracles; refers to Simon Kimbangu.

nzari (in-ZAH-ree): river; the origin of the Congo River's name during Mobutu's rule.

Soukous (SOO-koos): African rumba, a type of music that developed in Congo-Kinshasa.

Sua (soo-WAH): a pygmy tribe that lives in the Ituri Forest.

French Vocabulary

authenticité (OH-TAUNT-tee-see-TAY): Mobutu's 1971 campaign designed to promote nationalism in Zaire.

cuvette (coo-VET): saucer or shallow bowl; refers to the Congo River basin.

le Grand Maître (LUH grahn MAY-truh): Great Master; refers to Franco Luambo.

pillage (pee-YAHJ): pillage; a two-day riot and looting spree in 1991 during which much of Kinshasa was destroyed.

secouer (SEH-coo-eh): to shake.

English Vocabulary

accolades: awards; tributes.

austere: simple and unadorned.

cassava: root used as a staple food in Congo-Kinshasa; also called manioc.

cassiterite: the chief source of metallic tin.

circumcision: the act of removing the fold of skin covering the genital organs of males or females, especially as a ceremonial or religious rite.

cobalt: a hard, silvery-white metal used to harden steel and produce a blue dye.

communist: relating to the system of social organization based on common ownership and equal distribution of property.

deploy: to organize and position troops, resources, or equipment to be ready for immediate action.

endemic: belonging to or native to a particular region.

epiphytes: plants that attach themselves to other plants and take nutrients they need from the air.

erratic: having a lack of consistency; irregular.

fetishes: objects that are believed to have magical powers.

genocide: the deliberate and systematic extermination of a racial, religious, political, or cultural group.

hydroelectricity: the generation of electricity from waterpower.

indigenous: originating in or characteristic of a particular region or country.

initiation: the ceremonies or rites of acceptance into a certain group.

insurrection: an act of rising up or openly rebelling against an established government or authority.

lineage: the line of descendants of a particular ancestor; family; race.

lingua franca: a language that is widely used as a means of communication among speakers of other languages.

navigable: describing a body of water deep and large enough to allow ships to pass through it.

nomadic: describing a person or group that moves from place to place in search of food or pasture.

nuclear family: a social unit consisting of a father, a mother, and their children.

Paleolithic: characteristic of the earliest phase of the Stone Age, which began in about 2,000,000 B.C.

Pan-Africanism: the idea that all African countries should make alliances with one another.

polygamy: the practice of having more than one spouse, especially a wife, at one time.

punts: moves a boat along a river by standing in the boat and pushing a long pole against the bottom of the river.

reneged: went back on one's word.

sanctions: measures taken by a state to restrict trade and official contact with a state that has broken international law.

savannas: plains characterized by coarse grasses and scattered tree growth, especially on the margins of the tropics.

seceded: withdrew formally from an alliance, federation, or association.

stronghold: a place that acts as the center of a faction or of any group sharing certain opinions or attitudes.

transcends: goes beyond the ordinary boundaries or limits.

More Books to Read

By the Grace of God: A True Story of Love, Family, War, and Survival from the Congo. Suruba Ibumando Georgette Wechsler (New Horizon Press)

Congo in Pictures. Visual Geography series. (Lerner)

Democratic Republic of the Congo. Cultures of the World series. Jay Heale (Marshall Cavendish)

Dikembe Mutombo: Mount Mutombo. Sports Stars series. Philip Brooks (Children's Press)

Exploration of Africa. Great Explorers series. Colin Hynson (Barrons Juveniles)

Gorillas in the Mist. Dian Fossey (Houghton Mifflin)

The Kongo Kingdom. African Civilizations series. Manuel Jordan (Franklin Watts)

Mbuti. Heritage Library of African Peoples. Onukaba Adinovi-Ojo (Rosen Publishing Group)

The Okapi: Mysterious Animal of Congo-Zaire. Susan Lyndaker Lindsey, Mary Neel Green, and Jane Goodall (University of Texas Press)

Stanley and Livingstone and the Exploration of Africa in World History. In World History series. Richard Worth (Enslow)

A Walk through a Rain Forest: Life in the Ituri Forest of Zaire. David Jenike and Mark Jenike (Franklin Watts)

Videos

Hidden Congo: Forest Primeval. (Questar)

Wildlife International — Zaire: Tracks of the Gorilla. (Tapeworm)

Web Sites

holly.colostate.edu/~shadow32/mbuti.html

www.africaguide.com/country/zaire

www.congo-pages.org/welcome.htm

www.infoplease.kids.lycos.com/ipka/A0198161.html

Due to the dynamic nature of the Internet, some web sites stay current longer than others. To find additional web sites, use a reliable search engine with one or more of the following keywords to help you locate information about Congo-Kinshasa. Keywords: *Congo River, Ituri Forest, Laurent Kabila, Kinshasa, Mobutu Sese Seko, mountain gorillas.*

Index